3 9082 13307 9460

√ 10/17 1L12/16

D0560819

The
Golden
Apple

The
Golden
Apple

Redefining Work–Life Balance *for a* Diverse Culture

Mason Donovan

First published by Bibliomotion, Inc.
39 Harvard Street
Brookline, MA 02445
Tel: 617-934-2427
www.bibliomotion.com

Printed in the United States of America

Library of Congress Cataloging-in-Publication Data

Names: Donovan, Mason, author.
Title: The golden apple : redefining work-life balance for a diverse
  workforce / Mason Donovan.
Description: Brookline, MA : Bibliomotion, Inc., 2016. | Includes index.
Identifiers: LCCN 2016024741 | ISBN 9781629561141 (hardcover : alk. paper) |
  ISBN 9781629561165 (enhanced ebook)
Subjects: LCSH: Work-life balance. | Diversity in the workplace. | Corporate
  culture.
Classification: LCC HD4904.25 .D6655 2016 | DDC 650.1—dc23
LC record available at https://lccn.loc.gov/2016024741

Dedicated to my dear friend Asha Marina Brouwer.
Life is simply better and more balanced with you in it.

Contents

Foreword

It is not uncommon to hear a CEO or business leader give a speech to the team and say, "We are a 'People First' organization, and people are our number-one asset." It is the politically correct thing to say and is generally widely accepted. This declaration will usually bring a round of respectful clapping from the team, and the leader and the leadership team will give one another approving nods and smiles, having confidence that they have checked the box to be a "People First" organization. "See, we value people," they think...but do they really?

The proclamation that "people are our first asset" is not a true reflection of a People First organization. People are not an asset! They live, they breathe, they are emotional, they think, and they feel whether their leaders truly value them, rather than just accepting what the leadership team says about them. They have lives in and out of the office, lives that require balance to reach their fullest potential. Brands, operational capabilities, physical tools—these are the assets of the organization. People are much more. They are the heart and soul of the company! They are the brains, the passion, and the will of the company! The people contribute the unique characteristics of your organization, and they are what makes it work or not, what makes the business sustainable or not! These unique attributes must be

embraced and celebrated. For without highly passionate, committed, purposeful, and soulful people, the company itself will
cease to exist.

In my experience, the only successful way to build and sustain—or transform—a business is to engage and empower purposeful people by motivating their "heads" and inspiring their
"hearts." Understanding what truly moves and inspires your
team, as individuals and as team members, and aligning them
with the company's purpose is vital to achieving this ambition
of a company that acts from both "head and heart." What are
the unique talents of your teams and their members? Do you
recognize, appreciate, and embrace their uniqueness? Do you
and your leadership team truly dedicate your time to knowing
and listening to your team, whether business is good or bad?
Do people really come first? They must; and we must go way
beyond just saying it, to achieve a motivated, dedicated, and
inspired "head and heart" organization. Our partnership with
the Dagoba Group directly connects to this "head and heart"
philosophy.

Each person in your company brings unique talents,
thoughts, and passions to your team and organization. Embracing, appreciating, and respecting these unique characteristics
are essential to attracting, building, and growing a diverse,
empowered team. Even though you may not fully understand
each colleague's uniqueness, you need to embrace and respect
all employees in your organization. Doing so requires that
many of the executives show strong leadership. The ability to
genuinely listen and engage people are near the top of the list of
traits leaders must have. Leaders must be dedicated to proximity
and availability, and must show a willingness to give of themselves to serve the team and its members. Also, they need to
have an unwavering commitment to building trust and forming

genuine, authentic, trusted relationships. When presented with people challenges such as work–life balance, we must seek out inclusive solutions that value our uniqueness while also embracing our shared goals.

So how do we build trust? Trust is not built with a great speech delivered from a podium! Trust is not something you can just ask for and receive! Trust is earned through everyday actions, both big and small. Trust is earned by genuinely caring, giving of oneself, and listening to what people are truly passionate about...their purpose. When you have this type of consistent approach and a relationship built on mutual trust, which truly takes time to build and is far harder to build than to break down, you will be embracing and elevating your team's uniqueness and be building a diverse team. Why? Because people are respected and appreciated for who they are and not simply as "assets."

There are many critical factors that will help you build trusting relationships with a diverse and inclusive team. Here are some of those traits:

1. **Authenticity.** No leader is perfect or without bad moments or emotions. We are all human. Yet a leader who is true to his or her values and beliefs can be trusted. Self-awareness and humility become great guides that can help us through our journey. If leaders can look themselves in the mirror each and every day, and say, "I did what was best for the team, no matter the difficulty," they have remained true to their values and are genuine.

2. **Recognition of both the privilege and the responsibility that a leadership role affords.** Having the opportunity to lead others in any capacity is a tremendous privilege, which allows us to make an impact, good or bad, on other people's lives. How

many times have you heard someone complain about his boss: "He doesn't know what he is doing," "She doesn't listen to me," or "He doesn't understand or respect me"? These sentiments are made because most leaders (bosses, as they see themselves) don't understand the flip side of their privilege, which is the responsibility to lead: the responsibility to set an example, and to give respect as they themselves want to be respected. Leaders have the opportunity to set an example by embracing diversity and including everyone. This is both a great privilege and a responsibility.

3. **Leadership from the head and the heart.** As I mentioned earlier, to bring true change and to transform organizations and people, we must motivate the intellectual element of the team and inspire people to genuinely care and believe in the company's mission and purpose. Leaders need to set a vision, make it clear to everyone, and communicate, communicate, and communicate. But the vision will never be achieved unless the team embraces and lives it. So leaders must set the example for the culture and environment they wish to create. They must live the values and exhibit the behaviors that create an atmosphere in which individuals can grow, thrive, and be themselves. This culture must be inclusive and diverse to attract long-term, highly committed, and passionate, purposeful people.

These three traits of leadership represent a few examples rather than an exhaustive list, but they are integral to forming the right kind of culture within any organization that seeks to embrace individual and collective uniqueness. And with this culture of trust in place, we can build a diverse and inclusive team, one that is unified, motivated, inspired, purposeful, and soulful, and that celebrates each individual for his or her special talents and contributions to making a winning team in business, society, and life.

The Golden Apple embraces these three traits as it tackles the work-life balance challenge present in today's rapidly changing workplace. This book will provide the reader who is struggling with this challenge for the first time or a long time, with a valuable resource to craft an effective strategy.

Cheers and best regards,
Nick Krzyzaniak
General Manager, Danone
Danone CIty Unit and Manifesto Catalyst,
Danone North America

Preface

The diversity and inclusion conversation is changing from one that is separate and focused on differences to one that integrates core challenges and is tied to inclusion. Competitive marketplaces are forcing organizations to be more reflective, and less reactive, to people challenges, whether these are internal or external. Three major obstacles are on the CEO's desk at any one time: innovation, employee and customer engagement, and work–life balance. The latter of the three has an inordinate impact on the first two, and thus needs to be addressed first. The available skilled labor pool is shrinking relative to demand. Tie that small pool of qualified candidates to immense budget restraints, and corporations find that more is required from fewer employees. Without a culture that is designed for presence and balance, these companies will receive a depreciating return from their staff. Leaders who are not developed to achieve their own healthy work–life balance will never be able to model it for their teams.

Work–life balance is a people challenge, and thus inclusion must be part of the solution path. Gone are the days of one-size-fits-all solutions for one specific group of employees. Solutions must reflect a heightened awareness of diversity, and need to be inclusive. They also must have flexibility built in if they are to achieve the intended results. *The Golden Apple* is a primer for all organizations and leaders that truly want to start the path toward a healthy workplace not only for their teams, but also for themselves.

In order for diversity and inclusion efforts to remain effective and relevant, they need to delve deeper into solving corporate core challenges. D&I can no longer simply be a separate conversation. It has to be part and parcel of any dialogue about people. At the same time, we cannot relegate the diversity topic to a back shelf. We still need to reduce unconscious bias and expose ourselves to difference, understanding the impact of insider–outsider dynamics and raising awareness of inequity. By taking a core challenge such as work–life balance and weaving an inclusive solution that encompasses diversity, we will move closer to a meritocracy that fully leverages all of our human capital.

Introduction

Accelerando and crescendo: a crash course in organizational music.

It might seem odd that the beginning of a book on work–life balance begins with a music reference. Personally, I have found that music soothes, energizes, annoys, haunts, or even exhausts me, much the way my work or personal life does. It is no wonder movie montages always have some musical score tied to the emotional theme they are trying to express. If you encapsulated my corporate existence into a montage, the musical score would probably start playing at an audible level when you see images of me in graduate school. Without a doubt this musical piece was in the background since I was very young, when I became aware of the economic differences between the haves and have-nots, but someone definitely tweaked the volume up when I enrolled for my master's degree in international business.

International marketing and cross-cultural team dynamics were all very exciting and interesting; however; it was a course that some may consider a monumental yawn, international accounting, that I found most alluring. Managing a smart flow of revenues and expenses across international borders, corporate business units, and their divisions was a feat of organizational and mathematical genius. One small move could result in a significant bottom-line impact. Layered on top of it all was the finite quantity of time. As a U.S. corporation, paying your euro-based expenses in the morning when the U.S. dollar is strong while transferring your euro-based revenue later in the day when the dollar is weaker was a winning combination. The opposite was true for corporations based in Europe. Understanding where and when this revenue had to flow in order to mitigate tax implications was also key.

It wasn't until later in my life that I realized that, although I was fascinated by the process, my passion was with the people involved in the process. Whole armies of people were and are devoted to taking advantage of this process in commodities, exchange markets, and tax mitigation, to name a few areas. These people had to be not only smart, but quick. Actually, they just had to be a bit smarter and a little quicker than the next person. Finance did not have this competitive flow process to itself; on the contrary, the process of being just a little better than the next group was replicated in one way or another in every part of the organization.

Before I knew it, I was dancing to the same ever-increasing pace of corporate music. Looking back, it was a group dance. Each of us hungry business grads was trying to outdo the next one. Our leaders at the time were our professors, some of them hailing from a well-connected business past. We wanted to impress them, so we read more; wrote bigger, better, more distinctive dissertations; and generally found ourselves moving to a quicker beat. The pace was too fast for some, as they let the candle go too long and bright, and burned out early.

As with a favorite childhood rondo, we would sing a verse and then do it a little bit harder and a little bit quicker until we got to a point when the pace would outstrip our abilities, and we ended in a chaos of exhaustion and laughter. A business rondo would repeat in neat, ordered timings, such as each quarter or each fiscal year. For example, sales staff are expected to not only repeat their previous success but surpass it (a little bit harder and a little bit quicker). The music got ingrained in our corporate way of life. I was no exception. As members of generation X, we were the first to break the lifelong commitment to one company. Many of us saw our parents either stuck at one level or laid off. In order to achieve bigger, better, and more our generation started the job-hopping movement. Each move to a new company had to bring a higher title and pay. Each pause between these hops needed to be shorter than the last. This pace is replicated by millennials, and has even increased, for they are quick to leverage digital tools to accelerate. Why use a phone to talk when texting is so much quicker? Why bother to form four or five relationships, when social media can help you manage hundreds? Speaking to a group seems like a waste of time when your tweets can reach thousands or even millions.

As I moved from sales associate to sales manager to director and so on, my personal life mirrored the pace. For a twenty-year period, I did not live in one place for more than nine months. My father would say he had two address books, one for me and one for everyone else. My bank account and closet grew with each new step. The way I measured success was either consciously or unconsciously passed on to those I influenced. Who wanted to keep up with the Joneses when they could *be* the Joneses? Work bled into my home life in the form of early-morning meetings followed by late-night catch-up or proposal writing on a Saturday instead of going to that festival I had been looking forward to. One-time exceptions quickly became the rule. My work even seeped into my dreams, waking me up covered in sweat with a thousand thoughts racing through my head. Lack of sleep caused me to have a shorter temper both at work and outside of work. Although I would not have admitted it at the time, my ability to innovate, be reflective about my decisions, and maintain the mental patience needed to learn other points of view all suffered. Due to these diminishing capacities, I relied more on an ever-smaller circle of friends and colleagues. So this was my accelerando, a musical term for a quicker and quicker pace, and my crescendo, another musical term for playing the notes with increasing emphasis. However, the pace is all relative. When the organizational music is playing harder and faster relative to yours, you don't realize your speed until you stop.

For some, stopping can be tragic, as was highlighted in a June 1, 2015, *New York Times* article, "Reflections on Stress and Long Hours on Wall Street." Between 2013 and 2015, the banking industry had experienced a rash of deaths connected to work and the lack of a healthy balance over the long term. A minority of employees, those with greater self-awareness, simply make the smart choice to step aside. And then there are the rest of us, for whom their entire existence can come crashing down in one sad moment. That moment for me was in the Albany airport. I had been flying out week after week on Sunday and coming home on Friday, visiting two or three cities and a multitude of staff and clients. As the saying goes, I was running on fumes. One week, a Friday meeting finished early so I rushed off to the airport to catch an earlier flight home. I patted myself on the back for making it in time to switch tickets and grab a fast airport dinner. There I was, sitting at my assigned gate gobbling down my nondescript cellophane-wrapped sandwich, when I looked up and noticed nobody was at the gate anymore. Odd, I thought, as I did not hear any gate call. I tossed the remains of my meal in the trash and peered up at the monitors. My gate had changed. With my rollaboard in tow, I rushed to the new gate, only to catch a glimpse of my plane home pulling away from the gate and onto the runway.

I wanted to scream, "Come back!" I wanted to use every swear word in the book. My mouth opened and nothing came out. My hands grew slack, sending my bags tumbling to the floor. I sat down right there on the floor in front of the ticket podium in my brand-new suit. Sounding like a broken *Wizard of Oz* record, I kept repeating to myself, "I just want to go home." I was done. I was spent. This was my subito pianissimo, the musical equivalent of a full stop. There was an eerily disconcerting silence. Although the airport intercom was probably still blaring announcements, I did not hear them. It was as though my sense of hearing had been turned totally inward. My heart was beating slowly and deeply. My thoughts were as loud as spoken words. Random images of me in hotels, airports, and taxis, rushing to or from meetings, spilled in front of my eyes. I started to ask myself a number of questions, which would not be answered right there and then. Why am I here? What am I doing? Where is this all leading? Why does it matter?

My knee-jerk emotional reaction was to find a way to quit everything and seek out any life that was the opposite of the one I was leading. Having browsed a few "work–life" books in the airport, I knew the answer was always about leaving work, in some fashion, and discovering some new personal life. I put the term "work–life" in quotations because these self-help gurus seem to think there is work and then there is life. I never understood how they made this separation. Regardless of your profession, work is very much part of your life. Also, most of the books made work seem to be the ill of humanity. From where I stood, work in and of itself was not an inherently bad thing. The real challenge was developing a healthy and fulfilling pace that aligns our work and our personal, at-home lives. I, and many of you who are reading this, may have had the proverbial golden handcuffs, which make us feel trapped in our work rut because we are held by the promise of future rewards. We expanded our debt each time our compensation expanded, requiring us to work that much more. Our attention is so focused on the eventual rewards—rewards that are a quarter or a year out, or possibly as far away as retirement—that we lose sight of today. In my eyes this paradigm shift was really about exchanging those golden handcuffs for a way of life that allowed health, wealth, and well-being yet didn't leave the gold behind. The title of this book was based on that something else, which I call the Golden Apple. We do not need to leave our jobs or give up those rewards, but we do need to redefine our work and personal lives to get a bite out of that apple. The apple is a symbol of health, wholesome life, and knowledge. I could not think of a better symbol to use for finding that healthy balance. To keep it top of mind I conclude this book using the word "apple" as a mnemonic to help remind you of five important themes to finding that satisfying balance.

Let me first define what I mean when I talk about a healthy work–life balance: it is simply developing a rhythm that will allow you to be present where you are (whether that is at work or at home) and to obtain fulfillment from both sides. The emphasis should be on the balance. I have spoken to many people who knowingly spend needless hours at the office to escape from their personal lives. When they are at home, they escape by burying themselves in a laptop or on their mobile device. On the other end of the spectrum are those who dread coming to work, and develop behaviors that divert their attention throughout the day into their personal lives, such as constantly monitoring Facebook or texting endlessly with anyone who will reply.

Life without work sounds like a dream to many until they are lucky enough to experience it. According to a WebMD article based on a Shell Oil study, "People who retire at 55 are 89%

more likely to die in the 10 years after retirement than those who retire at 65." We need work in our lives. We are all happier when we are working with a purpose. Now, that purpose may not be found in the job you have had for the past ten years, but balance does require leisure on one side of the scale and work on the other.

Companies long ago realized balance was important, and they created policies to provide at least a modicum of balance, such as mandatory vacation leave, flextime, job sharing, and parental leave. All of these policies, which I will call written systemic norms, are meant to foster healthier, more productive employees. Some companies, such as Microsoft, have extended these policies to their vendors. As a stipulation for doing business with the company, Microsoft requires its approximately two thousand vendors to offer fifteen days of leave to their employees. Why would they place this demand upon their vendors? My viewpoint is that Microsoft considers vendors with employees who have greater work and personal life balance as better able to provide them with superior products or services.

However, anyone who lives the corporate life knows that it's the unwritten systemic norms that reign king. The unwritten norms are the expectations, from management or the corporate culture, that are not found in any employee handbook. For example, my former employer had a written policy of unlimited vacation time for its sales staff. The idea was that, as long as you were meeting your sales quota, you were free to enjoy your time off. During the recruiting process, the unlimited vacation policy made a very attractive pitch. However, once on board, employees realized that the leadership culture did not look with favor upon anyone who took advantage of that policy even if they were meeting or exceeding all of their work goals. A vacation that lasted more than a few days would draw unwanted attention your way. It took a few years before the human resources department noticed a growing number of exit interviews in which the lack of time off was given as a top reason for leaving. Although the policy clearly stated that employees had vacation available to them as long as they were in good standing, the unwritten norm of a very competitive sales culture trumped the policy. A 2015 Lean In and McKinsey study found 90 percent of both men and women feared that taking advantage of a policy to provide greater work–life balance would hurt their position at work. A September 30, 2015, *Wall Street Journal* article, "Flexibility Is Great. But." detailed the same study, which found that only 12 percent of employees participate "in programs such as part-time or reduced scheduling or efforts aimed at smoothing maternity-leave transitions."

In chapter 4, I will go into greater depth about how we as leaders consciously or inadvertently foster and challenge a healthy balance. This book explores and provides perspective from both a leader's vantage and at a personal level. However, this book will concentrate specifically on how you as a corporate leader can influence and foster a workable balance that creates greater productivity, increased morale, and higher retention, and that provides a bottom-line impact. I do understand, too, that you may have limited resources (people and budget) and an expected output that requires maximum leveraging of those resources.

Although a 2013 Society for Human Resource Management study stated that 57 percent of U.S. corporations allowed for telecommuting, it should also be noted that my experience has shown policies such as work-from-home and work sharing are (1) not always feasible and (2) do not always provide the return sought. As a matter of fact, for some employees, working from home may create an even greater imbalance, as they find it difficult to separate work life from home life. Leaders will be frustrated if their employees' work life is hampered by uncontrolled personal life interruptions when they are not in an office environment. Companies like Yahoo, HP, and Best Buy have either eliminated or drastically curtailed their work-from-home policies.

The thrust of this book is twofold. First, it is aimed at you as a people leader, exploring ways you can influence or directly impact a healthy work–personal life culture given your organizational restraints (budget, staffing, marketplace requirements, policies, etc.). However, as a leader, the way you effectively manage the balance between your own work and personal life will resonate louder than anything you say. We will pay particular attention to managing the personal side of life. Combining effective personal life management with your day-to-day leadership actions will help you retain a highly productive and diverse team over the long term.

Second, this book will be speaking, for the most part, about larger firms—those with 10,000 or more employees. Should you give attention to work–life balance if you are leading a small to mid-size firm? The answer is a resounding yes. You have a smaller workforce to draw upon and thus fewer redundancies. If you should lose an employee or if the person's productivity simply drops due to a long-term work–life imbalance, the impact will be heavier. As a small business owner myself, I know that the fight to keep balance in a small organization is hard; you wear multiple hats and everyone relies on you to forge the path. Your business very often becomes your life, especially in the start-up phase. Dunbar's Law, established by British anthropologist Robin Dunbar, states that we have the cognitive faculty to manage a maximum of 150 relationships to maintain a stable, cohesive group. As you apply this law to organizations, you will find that 150 is the number at which a company must be broken into divisions and/or teams. As an example, sales departments actively organize their people into country zones, then regions, verticals, and local office teams. If this law is applied to a 10,000-employee company, CEOs are typically two or three levels removed from the frontline. It is at this level that I have found that organizational policies designed to manage a healthy workforce (e.g., inclusive leadership, work–life balance, etc.) require a more concerted and consistent approach to be successful. You can definitely apply the teachings in this book for smaller firms, including sole proprietorships; however, the research and stats provided are aimed at larger, multilevel organizations.

All that being said, I should give you a proper outline of the learning path you are about to take. Before you and I move into the "whats" and "hows," I believe it is important that you understand from a leadership and personal perspective why work–life balance is important. How is work–life balance impacting your health and well-being, personally, as well as the well-being of your team? By extension, how is work–life balance impacting your organization as a whole and your place in the market. You could call this chain of reasoning the business case for investing your resources in this subject.

After you have understood why the subject of work–life balance requires your attention, I will pull back the curtain to understand why this imbalance is happening. We will discuss how technology is changing our cultural learning behaviors. As I explore the subject from a corporate leadership perspective, you will be asked to consider how well-intentioned policies may have unintended impacts. Last but not least, this book will look at the influence work–life balance has on our hypercompetitive global environment.

In chapter 3, I go deeper, into an interactive exploration of purpose at four different levels. You and I will start together at the top, from the marketplace level, to flesh out your organization's overall value to its customers. We will then dive down to the systemic level, to better understand the purpose of your business unit. Taking one step further down, I will lay out your direct team's raison d'être. And finally, the book will look at your personal life and the reason you show up every day (or, possibly, the reason you don't). It may seem a simple exercise, but more often than not I find there is a serious misalignment at one or more levels, which creates undue stress and time sinks. As a leader, you will find it hard to create a healthy culture if you do not address all four levels.

The next two chapters, 4 and 5, go into practical, actionable detail on how to achieve that sought-after healthy work–life balance from a personal and leadership level. The first few chapters prepare you for the task in front of you in these chapters: to create an action plan that you can implement easily. Again, I will focus on small actions that can be immediately implemented so you can begin to see measureable results in the short term as well over the long term.

My professional interest in work–life issues was born out of my decades of work helping companies create an inclusive environment. I have seen how inattention to work–life balance creates a barrier to achieving diversity and inclusion goals. This is a pressing issue for you as a leader as you attempt to create market differentiation and expand into new markets. I have devoted a whole chapter to inclusion and how work–life balance can either foster or challenge this initiative. If it is a people challenge, inclusion should be part of the solution.

As with any initiative aimed at long-term change, sustainment is key. Chapter 6 looks toward systemic changes and check-ins that will help you and your organization craft a plan

that will last beyond the flavor of the month and promote ongo-
ing balance. As fast as technology changes, the demands for our
attention change. A sustainment plan must not only take your
current state into account, it must be flexible enough to adjust to
your future state.

The end goal is to be able to manage your corporate musical
score so that you can endure moments of accelerando (increasing pace) and crescendo (increasing demands), and avoid the
subito pianissimo (sudden stop). This is your song and your
orchestra. Create a chorus that brings harmony for yourself,
your team, and your company.

As I work with corporations around the world on this topic,
I am also in a learning mode, so I love it when you share your
successes or your challenges. Send your story to us at info@
TheDagobaGroup.com.

Chapter 1

Why Is Work–Life Balance Important?

A three-legged table will stand fine until it is leaned on all four sides.

During my first job out of college, I was renting a basement flat in Washington, D.C. I was living on an entry-level salary, so when I saw a table someone put out on the curb I snatched it. It was a nice table, with one minor fault: it was missing one leg. Propped up against the kitchen wall, it worked fine for breakfast and quick dinners. Then I had a couple of friends over. Long story short, a whole chicken and a bottle of wine ended up crashing to the floor. I look back on this incident when I think about how some of us fool ourselves that everything is fine. We spend long hours at work, and then when we come home we never really disconnect as we take phone calls and check e-mails. Because personal life is crowded out at home, it starts to play out in the office. We spend time texting friends and checking social media to keep up on what we missed because we were working when we were at home. Pressures build up, we struggle to disconnect, and stress slowly increases, affecting our sleep and life satisfaction. Unless we find a way to create balance over the long term, our proverbial three-legged table will eventually crash.

The Organization for Economic Cooperation and Development (OECD) has sought ways to measure the health of economies beyond counting dollars in and out via gross domestic product (GDP). The organization realized that GDP was not a be-all and end-all. It also knows there is much more behind GDP than a simple economic engine. As anyone who has followed the stock market knows, there are many factors that may seem unrelated to the stock but have a major influence on the stock price on a given day. Weather, political unrest, consumer confidence reports, and the price of fuel, as well as hundreds of other factors, play into corporate valuations as well as into a country's overall GDP.

After a massive amount of research, the OECD started the Better Life Initiative in 2011. This initiative was intended to provide another measuring stick for economic health, or possibly a predictor of future GDP. Of the eleven measured factors, which included housing, jobs, and education, one specifically measures work–life balance.

Among the OECD's thirty-four member countries, some common threads were emerging in the cultural zeitgeist. One of these was the desire among people to move up the hierarchy of needs, as defined by psychologist Abraham Maslow, from maintaining basic physiological needs such as food, shelter, and security to attaining happiness and a sense of purpose. Some found this in acquiring more food, shelter, and security, but the law of diminishing returns figured heavily. A second and third house, for example, provided a thinner margin of happiness and for a shorter period of time. We could only eat so much food in a day, and more exotic fare is not exotic once everyone else is eating it too. Societies that had their basic needs satiated were asking themselves, "What else?"

Businesses found that increasing salaries or inflating titles worked to engage employees, but at a critical level of satiation that strategy also fell prey to the laws of diminishing returns. Furthermore, there was a limit to what corporations could provide to their entire employee population and still deliver the expected value demanded by shareholders. In the world of tech start-ups, where cash is often a scarcity, employers offered other sticky aspects, such as innovative work space, convenience in the form of onsite services (e.g., laundry services, child care, gyms, hair salons). They also allowed employees to devote time to their passions; Google's 20 percent time is one such example. This program allowed employees to devote 20 percent of their time to special projects that may not fall directly within the purview of their jobs.

Productivity

Why would organizations invest in areas that seem primarily connected to providing a greater balance between work and personal life? The first answer is productivity. In order to provide greater returns, corporations are charged with getting more from the same, or even better, from less. This charge means that they need to produce more without increasing the number of people they employ. For some companies, this has meant having their employees work longer hours. However, longer hours did not always mean greater productivity per employee, because people's production value per hour may decrease as they work longer hours. In *BusinessWeek*'s article "The Increasing Call for Work-Life Balance," they note a Corporate Executive Board (CEB) survey of fifty thousand global employees found that those employees who felt they had a better work–life balance worked 21 percent harder than those who didn't. In addition, the Federal Reserve Bank chimed in with a study showing a healthy work–life balance increased productivity by more than 10 percent. In a separate study, *Impact of Extended Overtime on Construction Labor Productivity,* Awad Hanna, Craig Taylor, and Kenneth Sullivan noted that construction projects that required a long duration of sixty-hour weeks realized a productivity average about 24 percent less than similar projects on which employees worked forty-hour weeks. If we were to extrapolate from either of these studies' productivity results to what would be needed to get more out of an employee by methods such as increasing hours worked, the cost–benefit case is quite clearly in favor of investing in leadership development on work–life balance.

The case may be clear for some, at any rate. The same CEB survey found that 60 percent of HR executives polled felt satisfied with the work–life services at their organization, while only 16 percent of the employees felt the same way. This margin indicates a major disconnect, underlining the point I made about written and unwritten norms in the introduction to this book. If you recall, the written policy at my former employer allowed unlimited vacation time, while the unwritten norm expressed by management culture frowned upon vacations that lasted longer than a week. If you asked HR representatives about the work–life offerings at the company, they probably would have given a high score, not realizing the written policies were superseded by unwritten norms. To underscore this point, the 2014 Glassdoor Employment Confidence study revealed that the average U.S. employee uses only half of his earned vacation time. Of the employees who do take vacation, 61 percent report working on vacation.

It should be abundantly clear that productivity is a major factor for the success of any company, and it is hampered or bolstered by the company's work–life culture. What would a simple 5 percent increase in productivity mean for your team, business unit, or organization?

Innovation

Another key driver for any organization's success is its ability to stay relevant and fresh in the marketplace. Or, in three words: innovation, innovation, innovation. Face it, with a global economy that is virtually connected, large organizations are finding they must compete with everyone, everywhere. The demise of the newspaper industry offers a fine example. The Internet has created hundreds of thousands of individual reporters who vie for local or national attention. Paying and waiting for the morning newspaper fell out of favor, as readers could choose their digital channel, which sourced everything immediately at their fingertips. Innovation is required for long-term success, and innovation comes from one source: your people. When was the last time you saw robust innovation from a group of tired, overworked employees? A 2011 University of Pennsylvania sleep study found the primary exchange of hours for sleep was work, meaning that increased work hours were directly related to fewer hours spent sleeping. Less time available outside of work was not a withdrawal from other personal activities. Less sleep means a less alert and thus less innovative employee.

Goldman Sachs's 2011 report *Innovation and Economic Growth* connects a nation's economic success with its ability to retain an innovative workforce. Marketplace common sense tells us that today's principal player (i.e., MySpace) can lead quickly to the next innovation (i.e., Facebook). Companies have two major avenues for innovation. First, they can purchase another innovative firm. This is a common strategy among cash-rich organizations. Take the example above about Facebook usurping MySpace. In the first quarter of 2015, Facebook acquired three firms (Wit.ai, QuickFire Networks, and TheFind). In 2014 the social media company made eight acquisitions, with WhatsApp probably the most well known. Because Facebook has more than 1.3 billion users at the writing of this book, I am going to guess that those acquisitions were not based primarily on a desire to acquire more traffic. These acquisitions provided Facebook with fresh, innovative tools that will allow it to remain relevant in today's finicky consumer space.

The second major path to innovation is from within. Corporations depend on their employees to generate industry-leading products and services. 3M is well known for its internally driven innovation, and its Post-it products are often cited as an example of the company's innovative culture. 3M has a rule that 30 percent of each division's revenue needs to come from products introduced in the past four years. I also mentioned earlier that Google's policies allowed employees to devote 20 percent of their time to non–job specific responsibilities, which helped drive innovation. These companies, and many others, have created systemic norms that emphasize innovation. However, even they are not immune to the impact of stressed-out employees who are burned out because of a persistent imbalance of work and personal life.

The annual *Work Stress Survey* conducted in 2013 by Harris Interactive for Everest College found that 83 percent of U.S. employees were stressed at work. On the top ten list of stressors were a heavy workload and poor work–life balance. In addition, a Graham Lowe Group Canadian study, "Control Over Time and Work–Life Balance: An Empirical Analysis," found that 60 percent of employees surveyed experience work–family conflict, when role overload was considered. Companies have always been looking to do more with less, but since the 2009 recession, that goal has really squeezed staff. As layoffs occurred, many employees took on responsibilities in addition to those of their own jobs, causing longer work hours, more meetings, and generally greater challenges to maintaining a healthy, balanced workplace culture. Employees could likely handle extra responsibilities if there was lower demand for products and services. However, the economy started to rebound, increasing demand, while most companies were hesitant to increase staff to accommodate this renewed demand. This may explain the 10 percent increase in stress in the 2013 survey when compared with the *2012 Work Stress Survey.*

Customer demands grew while the staffing levels stayed fairly static, leading to a team that is struggling to keep its head above water. The company still needs to innovate, and if it is not able or willing to purchase innovation in the form of acquisitions, then it has to rely on its existing employee population. Organizations that want employee-led innovation but are not in a position to hire more staff to lighten the workload are realizing that they need to focus on instilling more balance into the daily lives of their teams. The knee-jerk reaction may be to think that the only path to healthier work–life balance is reducing workload. It is certainly one way, but it does not work for every employee and it is not always financially feasible for the organization. We will speak to simple and practical action plans in chapter 4, "Achieving Balance and Presence in Work."

Talent

We have touched on two core reasons, productivity and innovation, that work–life balance is important to organizations. The third may come as no surprise: talent. Whether you are acquiring new talent or trying to retain the best and brightest among your employees, the way your culture fosters a healthy work–life balance will impact your results. Having consulted for companies on talent acquisition strategies for more than a decade, I can tell you that the subject of work–life balance is common in recruitment literature. Also, as a founder of a global diversity and inclusion firm, I can tell you that the way these conversations are broached often depends on the demographics of the candidates. Work–life balance conversations come up far more often when leaders interview women than when they interview men. In the March 2014 issue of *Harvard Business Review,* the "Manage Your Work, Manage Your Life" article highlighted a five-year study of four thousand executives. One glaring finding was, "Executives of both sexes consider the tension between work and family to be primarily a women's problem." However, studies have shown that men are rating work–life balance higher on their list of factors they consider before accepting a job offer. A Families and Work Institute study, *Overwork in America,* showed a 25 percent increase in the number of men reporting stress related to workplace–family life balance, while the results for women stayed virtually flat. When asking client companies about their candidate pool, we often found the recruitment team deemed that, after compensation, work–life balance would be the top concern for female candidates and career advancement for male candidates. When actual candidate survey data was shown, our clients were surprised that in almost every circumstance women rated career advancement above work–life balance and men at times did vice versa. This reflected faulty but understandable unconscious biases based on gender.

A healthy balance between work and personal life was important to both men and women, but because of our conscious and unconscious biases, which show up in our assumptions, it is often still treated as a concern only for women. This disparity also found its way into generational hiring practices. When employers recruit candidates who are just out of college, work–life balance is not a common conversational topic. When employers make lateral recruits of those thirty to fifty years old, however, work–life balance concerns are put on the table immediately. The tendency is to think of work–life balance as an issue only for those who are more likely to have family demands. Although being a caregiver does put greater responsibility on an employee, family is not the only reason employees are seeking a healthier, more enriching life both in and out of work.

If you were, or know anyone who has been, recruited straight out of college and into a Big Four accounting firm, you've probably heard the phrase "churn and burn." The Big Four were notorious for hiring huge numbers of graduates and then putting them through grueling schedules of endless travel and long hours. Those few who did not burn out in the first couple of years had an opportunity to be promoted. Churn and burn was a rite of passage for these firms, a ritual that many companies across all industries still employ today when they hire employees from younger generations.

PricewaterhouseCoopers (PwC) discovered that its usual offering of good pay, career potential, and partnership prestige was not resonating as strongly with new college recruits as it had in the past. Given that the company predicted that by 2016 80 percent of its workforce would be millennials (born between

1980 and 1995), it decided to sponsor a study (*PwC's NextGen: A Global Generational Study*, 2013) to better understand the needs and wants of the younger generation. The first key learning was this: "Many Millennial employees are unconvinced that excessive work demands are worth the sacrifices to their personal life." Seventy-one percent of PwC's millennial workforce said their work demands interfered with their personal lives. In the past, this concern was assuaged with the big corporate carrot of promotional opportunities (our earlier-cited golden handcuffs phenomenon). However, there was a definite crack forming in this promise's allure. According to the report, 15 percent of the company's male employees and 21 percent of its female employees said they would forgo some compensation and delay promotions in exchange for fewer work hours. They were seeking gold, but in the form of an apple instead of the handcuffs. They wanted increased compensation with a more wholesome life experience, not to have to trade one off for the other. In the introduction of this book, I mentioned how many people feel as though it was an either-or choice: either put up with the handcuffs in order to gain the gold, or give up on a lucrative career in order to find balance. The golden apple, as noted, is about having both.

As PwC's report discovered, if the company did not craft a new and more attractive employer brand it would be severely hampered in hiring, and eventually in retaining, employees. Even as companies are spending millions to acquire and retain a diverse workforce, the work–life balance issue is creating a backdoor challenge to hiring a younger generation. To add fuel to this fire are some hard generational facts. According to AARP's article "Baby Boomers Turning 65," eight thousand people in the United States will turn sixty-five every day for the next twenty years. When organizations look to fill their jobs with the next generational cohort, they are going to be challenged, as the gen X population (of which I am a member) is approximately half the size of the baby boomer generation. Even if there is zero job growth, companies will see a 50 percent decline in talent inventory in this next generational cohort.

Holding on to the baby boomer population longer may not be a solid solution, because baby boomers feel that they paid their dues and want more out of life than a nine-to-five job. A 2005 Merrill Lynch survey, *The New Retirement Survey*, found that 42 percent of baby boomers would only take jobs that allowed extended time off for leisure. Then the economy and their retirement savings went into a downward spiral, changing their outlook temporarily. Although the Great Recession quieted the discontent around this issue, due to the lack of alternative employment, the improving economy and reconstituted nest eggs are unleashing that pent-up angst. Spherion's 2012 *Emerging Workforce Study* illustrated that 42 percent of employees who had companies that invested in work–life balance programs were more likely to stay five years or more. It is interesting and compelling that, both to retain some engagement from the baby boomer generation and to attract the millennial generation, today's employers need to invest substantially in understanding work and personal life balance.

So we've touched upon three major reasons that investing in work–life balance is important to the organization: productivity, innovation, and the recruitment/retention of talent. A *2015 Workplace Flexibility Study* by Workplace Trends and CareerArc, sums up these propositions nicely: when more than a thousand professionals were surveyed about their organizations' efforts to create more work–life balance options, 65 percent realized an improvement in employee retention, 87 percent reported increased employee satisfaction, and 71 percent noted higher productivity. The only question missing on this study was the impact of work–balance on innovation; we can surmise, however, that a happier, more productive, and more engaged workforce is likely to be more innovative. In fact, Gallup's extensive *State of the Global Workplace* 2013 study showed strong links between the level of employee engagement and a number of important key performance indicators that determine the success of the business. The greater the imbalance of work–life will only lead to greater disengagement to these success factors.

A Multifaceted Issue

Before I move on to the personal reason that work–life balance is important, I should note that, based on all the research listed in this chapter, work–life balance is impacting everyone, across generations, genders, and geographies. Work–life balance is far from just a gender issue. It creates challenges based on generational difference, cultural difference, religious difference, and other important aspects of diversity. Because of this fact, the ability of an organization to understand and address work–life balance has become a core challenge in creating a truly inclusive workplace.

Many people tend to think that inclusion is about addressing discrimination. But it is also about creating the right conditions for the full engagement of an increasingly diverse group of employees. Thus, it is important to reframe the issue, as many companies are still treating it as a niche problem for parents, women, or a specific generation. While these groups may face specific challenges, it is important that you don't allow unconscious biases to limit thinking and strategies related to work–life balance. A lack of balance, however, may impact these groups disproportionately, often due to a manager's unconscious bias. Leaders fail to offer stretch assignments that demand extra hours to women with children; on the other hand, they may automatically assume a younger hire will want to work sixty hours a week with the promise of a future promotion. Inclusion is a central challenge to the work–life balance issue, as well as a core solution. Since it is such a vital area and can have repercussions both ways, I will weave the inclusion theme throughout the book, as well as devote a specific chapter to inclusion.

Before you consider your group memberships, such as gender, caregiver, or generation, let's first consider why achieving a healthy work–life balance is important to you as a human being with a family, friends, personal aspirations, and a limited life span. Here are some sobering facts. In 2012, the Centers for Disease Control and Prevention estimated the average life span of someone turning sixty-five years old in the U.S. that year has an additional 20.5 years for women and 17.9 years for men. Although retirement ages are changing, sixty-five is still widely considered the milestone retirement year. If you started work right out of college at the age of twenty-two (many started earlier), then you would have forty-three years of work under your belt by the time you turned sixty-five. If you lived the average of nineteen more years, then you spent more years working than you did not.

These facts probably caused you to sink a little in your chair, especially if you feel like work is putting your personal life on hold. Some of you may see this as a balance, with almost a fifty–fifty split between employed and nonemployed time, if you look purely at years. This time-equality perspective is a limited view of work–life balance, though. One can be employed for the majority of her life and still have a healthy balance between work and family life. Balance in this sense is not about the actual time spent doing one activity or the other. When I speak of balance, I am specifically referring to the state of being in which you feel fulfilled in both your work and non-work lives. This sort of balance is potentially available for all of your years, both employed and unemployed, after retirement for instance.

Having either side out of whack can have a detrimental impact upon you personally. Leveraging the research I provided above on the importance of a healthy, balanced culture, I can very easily see a few pitfalls for your work side of life. If you are not engaged or mentally present at work, either because you are burned out or because your personal life is continually interrupting it, you will likely be less productive and innovative. Your ability to manage your team will be hampered and your hiring decisions won't be as sharp. Lower productivity means you have to work more to accomplish the same goals. Less innovation may mean you are passed up for promotions or lose out on top bonuses. Your lack of ability to retain or hire the best talent will eventually lead to a difficult conversation with your manager or shareholders. All of these aspects will undoubtedly filter into your personal life at some time.

The Personal Impact

The Mental Health Foundation in the U.K. conducted a survey that looked into how a poor work and family life balance impacted us personally. A full one-third of those who participated felt unhappy about the time they devoted to work, with more than 40 percent of employees neglecting their personal lives because of their workload. Long working hours had a direct emotional impact on the employees: 58 percent felt more irritable, more than one-third felt anxious, and more than a quarter of employees felt depressed. More time spent at work created a vicious cycle in which employees also spent more time during non-work hours fretting about work. The most alarming result of this study was that almost two-thirds of employees had experienced a negative effect on their personal lives, such as physical and/or mental health problems, difficult personal relationships, lack of personal development, and an overall poor home life.

The Health Advocate published the paper *Stress in the Workplace: Meeting the Challenge,* in which they noted that "according to the National Institute for Occupational Safety and Health (NIOSH), 60 to 90 percent of doctor visits are attributed to stress-related illnesses and symptoms." In a much older *USA Magazine* article, "Job Stress: America's Leading Adult Health Problem," Dr. Paul Rosch postulates that a whopping 75 to 90 percent of all visits to primary care physicians are related to stress. Job stress is the leading cause of stress for adults. It also has a secondary stress impact on those around us. The Institute for Cognitive and Brain Sciences and the Dresden University of Technology noted in their 2014 findings *Your Stress Is My Stress* that simply being exposed to a person who is in a stressful situation triggers stress responses in your own body. Much like smoking around others can impact their health, the stress you bring from work can stress out those at home, just as the stress you bring from home can stress out your coworkers. Even more surprising, the observers in the study, who were not part of the experiment, had more than a 25 percent increase in their cortisol levels (a chemical produced by our bodies when we encounter stress).

Think about the last time you observed, either up close or from afar, a harried, stressed-out employee manage a situation. Try to replay how he acted, his choice of words, tone, and volume. Remember how it made you feel? Now think about this person being your boss or even your direct report.

Stress is not always a bad thing. It can kick us into gear so we reach that unreachable goal. Some of us just seem to perform better in stressful situations than other people do. The problem is not in the occasional stressful situation; the problem is the chronic stress that comes with a continual inability to fully manage either your work or your personal life. This type of ever-present stress leads to real health problems ranging from tightened muscles and back and joint pain to heart attack and stroke. Work–life imbalance, stress, and health are all connected.

We already mentioned that the inability to maintain a healthy work–life balance can lead to irritability, anxiety, and depression. These symptoms lead to interrupted sleep patterns, poor eating habits, social withdrawal, and abuse of drugs or alcohol. Over time, these secondary factors take a toll on everything from your respiratory and cardiovascular systems to your central nervous and endocrine systems.

If these negatives aren't enough, remember the secondhand stress phenomenon. You can pass the consequences of these health issues on to your coworkers and loved ones. As a leader, you need to understand the impact of your personal stress on your team, and also how particular team members may create an unhealthy situation for the group. Even if a particular work–life balance program seems to benefit only one member of your team, think about how the lower levels of stress on that team member will have an overall positive impact on the group.

Let's review why it is important as an individual to fully consider the impact of a healthy work–life balance. Most important, as I just noted, are your own health and the health of those around you. Second are your career prospects and the potential of your direct reports. Last is your overall happiness. Who doesn't want to smile on her way to work and on her way home?

Forgive me as I anthropomorphize my dog for a moment. Sophie is one of those happy, loveable golden retrievers. Luckily, my work environment allows me to have her with me for most of my non-travel days. She is either curled up by my feet under my desk or sitting in a chair next to me. She is just as happy running up the stairs to go to work as she is heading out for our afternoon walk. When I get stressed I look at her calmness and am immediately reminded that life is short. Somehow sensing my stress, she inevitably rolls onto her back, exposing her belly, and gives a goofy smile. Of course, I have no choice but to give her a few rubs. At these times I realize that happiness, just as much as stress, is contagious. When we have happy, fulfilled colleagues we also feel happier and more fulfilled.

Culture also is a self-reinforcing system. Imbalance in one area begets imbalance in other areas. If you create a space where you can be fully present while at work, you will also promote being fully present while at home. A fully rested healthy individual is a more productive, innovative, and happier employee. Now that you understand why it is important for both corporate and personal reasons, I will delve into what to do, but before I do that you should understand how we as a society got to where we are today.

Discussion Points

- Think of a time you were overstressed at work, and consequently experienced an extreme imbalance with your life outside of work. How did this situation impact your feelings? Your productivity? How did it affect the way you treated your coworkers? How did it affect the way you treated friends and family?
- Contrast this experience with times when the balance has felt right. What is that like?

- Which groups of people (e.g., women, parents, etc.) does your company choose as the focus of its work–life balance solutions? What other groups of people in your company would benefit from greater work–life balance?

Takeaways

✓ A healthy work–life balance will pay dividends in increased productivity, innovation, and stronger talent.

✓ Work–life balance is not just a gender or generational issue.

✓ There is a strong link between your health and the achievement of work–life balance.

✓ Corporations have found that golden apples, a rewarding career combined with a balanced work culture, are a stronger indicator for employee retention and engagement than golden handcuffs.

Chapter 2

How Did We Get Here?

It is one big game of Simon Says.

S imon Says put your right hand on your head and rub your stomach with your left hand," I would command my eight-year-old friends. I would repeat this statement a few more times, switching what the left and right hands were doing, before I would go in for the kill. While telling them to put their right hand on their head and rub their stomach with their left hand, I would do the opposite. Or I would say nothing at all and make the action. Without fail, my friends followed my actions as their behavioral cue rather than what I was telling them to do, even though they knew the way to win the game was to follow the proper verbal commands. So goes the childhood game of Simon Says. Whether it is the Norwegian "Kongen befaler" or the Spanish "Simón dice," this game of following leadership commands in a group setting is played by children around the world.

Somewhere along the way as we grow older, we leave this game in our childhood. However, the nature of the game, its core psychological principles, never leaves us. If you have children, you may have used the phrase, "Do what I say, not what I do" a few times when you were trying to teach them good behaviors. "Floss every day," you might say. "But Dad, I don't see you floss every day," the retort would come back. At work, your manager may tell you to watch out for expenses right before he takes everyone out for lunch. As humans, we are more keen on watching and repeating behavior than we are on carrying out a verbal command when the leader's actions contradict that command. Dr. Albert Mehrabian, known for his research on verbal and nonverbal messaging, wrote about his 7%-38%-55% Rule. The rule focused on communicating feelings or attitudes, especially when the underlying messages contradicted the words the person was saying. For instance, saying you are happy in a monotone with your shoulders hunched and your head hung low would certainly be contradictory. The rule said the receiver of the message received 7 percent of the message from the words you used, 38 percent from the tone of your voice, and 55 percent from your body language. So 93 percent of the communication received was from sources other than words.

Leadership Imitation

There is a mountain of science that basically says we, as humans, are prone to imitate actions. Cecilia Heyes and Elizabeth Ray demonstrate this point in their Associative Sequence Learning model, laid out in 2000. In the paper "Actions Speak Louder than Words: Comparing Automatic Imitation and Verbal Commands," by Helge Gillmeister, there is a long list of research studies that all come down to basically the same result: we are more likely to imitate actions than we are to follow verbal direction. So in large organizations where management is trying to influence culture through verbal communication and by crafting policies, but is contradicting those policies with actions, management is essentially leading a big game of Simon Says, and the majority of employees will lose.

Now, imitation is not always a bad thing. It is wonderful when people are imitating productive behavior, but it is detrimental when the behavior being imitated is not conducive to the long-term success of the organization or the individual. It is hard to count the times I have heard management say something akin to the following: "I am exasperated. I gave an open forum talk to get our employees to do X. We coordinated a whole communication campaign that included e-mails, posters, and videos to get them to do X. Yet, the moment we turn around they do Y. What do we have to do to get them to do X?"

The problem in moving behavior from Y to X in this situation often arises because the employees fail to do what Simon says and instead do what Simon does. Having provided diversity and inclusion development for more than twenty years, our firm has seen this predicament often. For example, I consulted for the executive team of a manufacturing company that was trying to create a more diverse and inclusive culture. They hired a chief diversity officer and charged her with developing a diversity and inclusion strategy. They signed off on all her proposed initiatives, which included adding employee resource groups, e-learning, and leadership development. The only suggestion the executive team did not take her up on was going through development themselves, because they already saw themselves as believers in the diversity and inclusion effort; after all, they were the ones who created the D&I position and funded the programs.

So this executive team was doing a lot of what Simon Says, but nothing in their own behavior changed. The team was still a very homogeneous group, and the unconscious biases of the executives remained unconscious and fully functioning. When it came to talent acquisition, assessments, or rewards, they remained slanted toward a very narrow demographic. It was not until the clearly frustrated CEO was publicly lambasting one of his VPs for failing to live up to the diversity campaign goals when the CEO finally understood. The VP graciously accepted the dressing down and then said, "Honestly, I was doing just what you were doing. In the past year you have not selected a single woman for a hire or special project assignment. I thought that diversity stuff was all just window dressing for the lawyers because I heard you did not even bother to attend one of the workshops." This VP was simply imitating the behavior of the most senior person in the organization, a tactic that has long helped people move up the corporate ladder.

Evolution of Corporate Culture

Before I speak to how corporate culture factors into developing effective work–life balance behaviors, let's take a brief tour through the evolution of corporate culture. There was a time when work was your life and what you did defined you. Many even took surnames based on their profession, such as Baker, Smith, and Farmer. An agrarian society (one in which 50 percent or more of the population was employed in the farming industry) had nonexistent lines between work and family life. The farm, your place of work, was typically also where you lived. It was the family farm. You worked, ate, and slept seven days a week, 365 days a year, on the same acreage. There was no such notion as work–life balance. Around 1500 CE, city-states such as Venice, Florence, and Milan saw their populations grow, while the percentage of citizens dependent on farming declined. By the late 1800s, Western Europe and the United States had transitioned to a society that had less than half of the population categorized as farmers.

Even before societies changed from agrarian to industrial, corporations were recognized. Roman law in the first century recognized groups that owned property. As time moved on, corporations became more defined, better regulated, and larger in size. These corporations eventually cleaved the agrarian work–life model, which had been one entity, into two; attention was now divided between work and personal life. You left your home to go somewhere else to work and then left your workplace to enjoy your personal life. Eventually regulations were developed depending on the country you lived in that set maximum standard workweek hours, minimum work age, and retirement age. There were many reasons for labor regulations, among them that they allowed societies to fence off work from personal life. It is of special note that farms were often specifically exempted from many of these laws.

With approximately 98 percent of the labor workforce in the U.S. being nonfarm workers, a constant struggle between work and personal life has arisen. Because some corporations have employee populations as big as small cities, it is not surprising that words can easily get lost when superseded by actions. C-suite executives take on celebrity status and, like celebrities, their every move is observed and imitated. Here is a case in point for an actual celebrity: Michael Phelps, winner of the most Olympic gold medals, can speak all day about how you should treat your body and mind like a temple, but his words ring hollow when he is arrested for drunk driving. Companies capitalize on this "follow me" phenomenon by having celebrities publicly wear the clothes or use the products they make.

The moment the celebrities fall off the straight and narrow, the brands switch to the next hot celebrity. Their actions will speak louder than anything the marketing teams can generate in ads.

When leaders preach to their teams about "getting a life" and finding time for their families, but then send e-mails on Saturdays and hold late-night meetings, their words lose out in favor of their actions. But let's not put chronic work–life imbalances all on leaders' shoulders. There are many other factors that got us to this critical juncture.

As much as the corporate world has evolved, so have the methods we use to engage with the corporate world, and with our personal world, for that matter. Before widespread use of the telephone, when you left work there was virtually no way for your employer to reach you or for you to reach the office. The telephone allowed your employer to call you to ask a question or to see if you would work additional hours, or to alert you to a crisis that needed your attention. On the flip side, the telephone also allowed your family or friends to call you while you were at work to discuss personal emergencies or simply to talk. The phone was followed by the computer, the Internet, and then all types of smart devices. Along with these ever-present and ever-connected devices came the ability—sometimes accompanied by the compulsive need—to be in two places at once. How often have you seen a restaurant dining room filled with people who were there physically but you knew, by the concentrated stares into the blue glow of their iPhones, that they were mentally somewhere else? How about the last time you were in a training session at work and your neighbor was either sneaking peeks at his device under the table or overtly typing on his tablet? Whether it was the evolution of our work lives or the technology that allowed us to blend the boundaries, it became a lot more difficult to create a distinct separation.

Digital Device Explosion

Regardless of where on the planet you live, personal devices have descended like locusts to feed upon our attention. By 2014, Apple estimated it had sold more than 500 million of its smartphones, the ubiquitous iPhone. *eMarketer* estimates that by 2018, more than two billion people will be using smartphones; this constitutes more than one-third of global consumers. Statisa reports that tablet shipments were 220 million in 2013, 230 million in 2014, and 206 million in 2015; smartphones were estimated to be 1 billion, 1.3 billion, and 1.4 billion, respectively. In just these three years alone more than 656 million tablets and 3.7 billion smartphones were added to the market. This number does not consider mobile phones not deemed to be "smart," laptops, or any other devices (such as smart watches) that will be added to the mix.

As of 2015, the world's total population was estimated to be about seven billion. So it may be fair to say that these devices are likely being used by one-third to one-half of the world's population. Of course, that percentage will increase as the devices stream more to the younger and older age sets. In the corporate population, people are typically multiple device users. In 2012, a study by Wireless Intelligence, the research arm of the GSM, revealed that mobile device users in the U.S. owned 1.57 devices, compared with 1.85 for device users elsewhere in the world. Each device demands a separate stream of attention from you, like a hungry puppy. It is not uncommon for someone in the corporate world to own a smartphone, a tablet, and an e-reader such as a Kindle (or the Kindle Fire, a device that doubles as a tablet).

Compounding the number of devices are more than a million

applications (aka apps) that can be downloaded. Each app is desperate for the user's attention, with many of them sending out notifications throughout the day and night in an attempt to snag a few minutes of time. Some of these apps are intended simply to amuse, like the popular game Angry Birds, while others are supposed to make us more efficient, like Genius Scan. All users start off buying devices and downloading apps with good intentions, but plans sometimes go awry, as a participant in one of our workshops told us in the following story.

Gui's Story

Guillaume, also known as Gui, would not be considered a member of the early adopter crowd. He did not own a mobile phone until work required him to get one. He was a financial analyst for a Silicon Valley firm that was looking at acquiring a target competitor. Before he had his mobile phone, Gui was living what his wife called the Dolly Parton dream: he worked nine to five. For Gui, work began when he sauntered into the office and ended when he stepped onto BART (the San Francisco Bay Area Transport system). For the most part, his family and work life did not intertwine. With the exception of the ritual 2 p.m. call he received from his wife, Maria, each day to tell him she was on her way home, Gui's work had few interruptions from his personal life. He would often chide his wife, a high school teacher, for grading papers while they watched TV or for the after-school committee meetings she attended.

At work Gui was seen as a very conscientious worker who was reliable and on nearly everyone's good list. A project given to Gui would undoubtedly be done on time and with no drama, so he was given the job of leading the team that would assess the financials of the potential acquisition. His boss dropped a shiny new iPhone on his desk and said, "Welcome to the twenty-first century." Although Gui treated his lack of a mobile phone as a bohemian badge of honor, he had been more than a little interested in purchasing one. "I will use this to help me be more efficient at my job," he told himself. The first thing he did was download a bunch of financial apps and set up notifications to alert him to any movement of the targeted company's stock. A few times a day, the phone would beep with these alerts.

On his way home, when he would normally peer out the window of the train car and allow his mind to relax and transition to home life, he decided to try out the Angry Birds game he'd heard so much about. He was fascinated by the physics behind the game and killed hundreds of pigs before he realized he had missed his stop. His wife was happy he got the phone, and immediately took it to download WhatsApp and Facebook. "Now I don't have to tell you what is happening with our friends, you can just tap on the Facebook link and see for yourself," she cheered. They had a "couples" Facebook account, but Gui had never logged in before. At 1 a.m. the phone lit up and beeped, startling Gui awake. Gui stared at the blue screen for a few seconds before he realized it was a financial news alert, read it, and then tried to go back to sleep. It happened again at 5 a.m., but this time he decided to just get up and go jogging. He put on the Fitbit health tracker his mother had bought him for Christmas and downloaded the app. The Fitbit was practically useless without a smartphone, but now he would be able to track his movements.

Over the next several weeks, Gui added close to fifty apps to his phone, wore his fitness tracker religiously, and started being more connected everywhere. Instead of the ritual 2 p.m. call, his wife sent him WhatsApp messages throughout the day to let him know what was happening, often referring him to Facebook to check out something one of their friends posted. Gui became a regular contributor to Facebook and started his own Twitter account. During his downtime on the train or while waiting in line for coffee, he could respond to e-mail or check out Instagram photos of his friends' vacations or dinners out.

His daily newspaper and current book were replaced by his Kindle, so he had more room in his work bag for his devices. In his first few months on the acquisition project, Gui seemed to be always on. Never did an e-mail, whether about something critical or mundane, go unanswered for more than thirty minutes while he was awake. He felt more productive than ever before. His friends were amazed at his connectivity. No longer were there times during the day when he would go dark. Gui could be connected at work and at home, 24–7.

Gui found the new project took more time than usual, keeping him later and later at work. His fitness tracker would buzz to notify him of inactivity, but he felt more tired than normal. He received a notification about something from one his devices every few minutes. It was almost like having a nagging child always at his side.

The words "Gui" and "having a bad day," which had never before been used in the same sentence by his colleagues, came up more and more often as Gui came off as irritable and short-tempered from time to time. Although Gui was more "connected" to his personal group of friends and family through social media and messaging apps, he had less time to be with them in person. Maria bought him an iPad for his birthday so he wouldn't have to squint at the small phone screen all the time. This device was paired with his iPhone and he loaded it with more graphic-intensive apps. Dinners at home, which had once been filled with conversation about the day, became silent as both Gui and Maria remained engrossed in their devices; on more than one occasion they sent each other e-mails or messages while sitting at the same table. Now, when Maria graded papers after dinner, instead of sitting down to a book as he had done in the past, Gui took the time to review spreadsheets.

Gui's talent assessment came as a complete surprise to him. In the past, he'd always scored high, but this time around he had a number of average and one below-average score. He could not understand the assessment, since he felt he was putting in twice as many hours as he had in the past. He never went "dark" and was always reachable, sending off e-mails at all hours of the night and on weekends. The one below-average score was in the column labeled "Contributes to a Healthy Working Environment." In the comments section, his manager had written, "Constantly distracted, causes undue work outside of working hours, and contributes to office stress." It all sounded very familiar, as his wife was making similar comments.

"How did I get here?" Gui asked himself. He'd gone from star employee to average in less than a year while working harder than he ever had. Gui was more tired, less fit, and he had an overall lower sense of personal happiness.

Gui's work–life balance went from healthy to poor not because he worked more hours but because he became unable to be fully present. He mistakenly equated spending more time on work affairs with being more effective at work, and he tried to make up for not being present in his personal life during non-office hours by connecting with family and friends while at work. The result was that he was constantly distracted, trying to be somewhere he was not. It was not simply the addition of technology that got him to that point, although technology gave him the vehicle to carry out his new behaviors.

Gui traded downtime, such as his train ride home or

after-dinner reading, for busy device work, such as games and e-mails that could have waited until the next day. Less downtime meant his brain had less time to decompress. He traded focused time at work for a workday filled with constant personal interruptions from social media and messaging apps. He got to this state with all good intentions. Instead of allowing the devices to create a more simplified and efficient way of connecting, however, Gui let them become interrupters and time vacuums. He was spending significantly more time receiving and banking information than using it.

Gui is not alone in the information overload phenomenon. When you have access to data 24–7—and when some of this data calls for your attention aggressively with beeps, flashes, and alarms—your brain has little time to process and actually use the information. LexisNexis conducted a survey in 2010 that looked at white-collar workers globally. The survey showed that the average employee allocates more than half her workday to receiving and managing information instead of leveraging it for her job. Half of those workers admitted they were nearing a breaking point that would not allow them to handle any more incoming information. This survey looked at work data. Add to this work data all the personal data we now receive during the workday from social media, self-help, educational, gaming, and messaging apps, and it is no wonder we and many of our colleagues feel like we are overwhelmed at any given point in time.

Organizations are, in their simplest form, groups of individuals focused on a common goal. With for-profit corporations, the ultimate purpose is usually making a profit, or, in other words, providing a return to investors. Beyond this high-level purpose is a more qualitative client purpose most employees will connect to, such as "providing customers with a healthy life" for a pharmaceutical company or "securing financial stability" for a financial management firm. The individual data overload phenomenon can eventually translate to a fragmented sense of purpose for the entire organization. This happens first at the micro level, when a small group of individuals who feel distracted, overloaded by information, and overwhelmed by an unhealthy work–life balance gets distracted and goes off on tangents, losing track of their intended mission. This concept is encapsulated in the following story of an executive team-building field trip; this story is a compilation of several true stories. Shareholders and employees alike perceived the organization as one that was losing focus. The CEO, whom I will call Richard, felt as though his direct reports were too fragmented and acting as if they were all working for different companies, all with their own goals.

The Mountaintop Goal

The field trip was simple. The company executives were to go on a two-hour gradual hike up the mountain, have lunch, and hike back down. There was only one rule: they could not talk about business. No talk about clients, competition, the marketplace, or talent. This trip was meant to create team cohesion by letting the executives accomplish a fairly simple task together. The side goal was to allow them to get to better know one another as people rather than as titles with departmental responsibilities. The first twenty minutes went as planned. They discussed kids, education, and hobbies. They got to a vista point with an open area. Lana, the CHRO, pulled out her mobile to take a group photo. Paul, the CIO, whipped out his selfie stick and handed it to Lana so they could all be in the picture. She was so focused on getting just the right angle that she accidentally hit Paul in the head with the stick when he walked out of her view. After a bit of triage, they determined that Paul should walk back to the car to get some first aid.

The group wanted to send the photo to Paul so he would have it when he got to the car. Cell reception was not good enough at the site, so they looked around and saw an opening not too far off the path. Within five minutes they were at the spot and, as luck may have it, there was just enough of a signal to upload. Lana also posted the photo to Facebook. Thinking this was the last spot where they might have reception, Richard called a ten-minute break so everyone could quickly check in before they headed the rest of the way up the mountain. Ryan, the chief counsel, got some troubling news on a recent piece of litigation. It wasn't urgent, but because Richard was there he shared the news. The ten-minute break turned into thirty minutes. David, the chief sales officer, quickly checked his e-mail, updated his dream team picks, and then turned on the elevation app and headed up a nearby peak to test it. Noticing how deeply Ryan and Richard were embroiled in their talk, he started to wander off to another peak. Janice, the CFO, was an amateur birder, so she fired up an app that identified bird sounds and headed off in the other direction to follow a bird call she'd heard while coming up the trail.

Ferdinand, the PR officer, started to receive messages from his friends and family on WhatsApp, commenting about the Facebook photo in which he was tagged. After five minutes of back-and-forth jabs with friends talking about his rough day at work, Ferdinand started a conversation with Lana about whether she should take down the photo. He was not sure whether the executive team should be seen taking a day to hike when the company was dealing with image issues. They walked behind a grove of trees so as not to disturb Richard and Ryan. Not long afterward, Richard looked up and realized nobody was in sight. He thought maybe the others had started up the mountain already. Ryan figured it would be best to head back to the car, just in case they missed each other on the way up or down. Richard agreed and they started back down. Ferdinand and Lana finished their conversation ten minutes later and, to their surprise, discovered that Richard and Ryan were gone. They supposed Ryan and Richard had gone to check on Paul and decided to join them at the car.

David and Janice both wandered so far off the path in their individual hobby pursuits that they got lost and independently concluded it would be best to just head down the mountain until they could find home base and start again.

Two hours into the hike, all the executives ended up back at the parking lot. Richard looked at the team and said mockingly, "How the hell did we all get here?" The group had one simple task with a common goal. However, they allowed themselves to be distracted by their gadgets and one another, as well as to be mentally elsewhere—and this precisely replicated not only their time at work, but also their time at home. Their purpose, a simple one, for that day was lost.

Now, imagine that they were leading their teams up that mountain. Although, as leaders, they may have given their teams the goal of reaching the top, how many members of their teams would imitate their actions rather than listen to their words? Life has certainly shifted since the agrarian period. We are torn between our personal and work lives. For many of us with families, there is no option for one parent to manage household work, so we try fit it into our workday and vice versa. Tools that were created to help us be better connected and more efficient allowed us to be more disconnected and less present. Our leaders, apps, families, social media, and myriad other inputs have become an overwhelming legion of "Simons." Now you know how we got here, but it is not where we have to stay.

Discussion Points

- Is it getting harder to accomplish both your personal and work goals? What distracts you?
- What distracts your team? Organization?

Takeaways

- ✓ Actions speak louder than words.
- ✓ Digital devices are not the reason for an unhealthy balance; they are just a conduit.
- ✓ Being present means limiting distractions and focusing on your purpose.
- ✓ Personal life can interfere with work life and vice versa.
- ✓ Personal devices have descended upon us like locusts, feeding upon our attention in and out of work.

Chapter 3

Finding Your Purpose

Even a rowing team needs a coxswain to remind them to row.

In the previous chapter, you read about Richard and his team on a simple team-building trip. Their inability to focus as a group on the hike was a mirror to the way the company was being fragmented. Each individual was constantly distracted and losing sight of his purpose. It is only when you discover your purpose that you are able to determine whether your behavior and activities support that purpose, allowing you to start decluttering your path to your goal.

When they don't pay conscious attention to purpose on a regular basis, teams and whole organizations become misaligned. Purposes should be simple and straightforward. It is easy to fall into the PR gobbledygook of corporate speak. For example, an engineering company I will call Engineering Firm #1 recently wrote out its purpose as "To deliver exceptional client experiences throughout the relationship life cycle," when its real quantitative purpose was "To generate a profit" and its qualitative purpose was "To design safe bridges that connect communities." Any for-profit company's main quantitative purpose tends to be generating a profit. How it generates profit (its qualitative purpose) will differ from company to company. Engineering Firm #1's purpose statement was really a supporting factor for its primary purpose, but even that could be easily simplified to something like, "To make clients happy." Happy clients tend to stay and spend more money.

But you may be asking, what does purpose have to do with achieving a healthy work–life balance? Well, if, like Richard and his team, people don't clearly recognize and stick to their purpose, everyone eventually wanders in their own directions, creating opportunities for distraction and making additional work to return to the starting point. If we take Engineering Firm #1's purpose statement as an example, every team could define exceptional client experiences in a different way, while some teams—such as HR, finance, or IT—that are not client facing may not even see themselves as supporting this purpose. Even if they were to all have a clearly defined purpose, they would eventually lose their way if they were not kept aware of the purpose and the intended alignment. Discovering purpose is valuable in developing a clear sense of direction. It is only then that you can solve what I call the sudoku puzzle exercise. Sudoku is a numbers game based on the process of elimination. Once you determine all the numbers that cannot fit in the square, you are left with the answer.

If Richard's team declared their purpose before the hike— for example, to reach the peak together within two hours—they could have put their actions into the sudoku engine. Did taking pictures help them fulfill their task? No, so eliminate it. Did determining their current altitude support their efforts? No, eliminate it. Would checking e-mail assist them in reaching the peak any sooner? No, eliminate it. Discovering your purpose allows you and your team to be more present for the task at hand. Keeping your purpose top of mind by posting it or having regular discussions will help everyone stay in alignment.

When I speak of alignment, I am really talking about purposes at multiple levels. First is the systemic level. What is the primary purpose of your company? As I mentioned earlier, if your organization is a for-profit company, I would wager the primary quantitative purpose is to generate profit or similarly generate value to shareholders, and the primary qualitative purpose is your expertise, why your clients look to you. Generating profit means taking in more revenue than you spend. Everyone in an organization can understand and align with this purpose. Either you are reducing expenses or you are generating more revenue. Easy, eh? It does seem easy, but, surprisingly, organizations get distracted from their primary purpose.

The qualitative purpose, which is more engaging to an employee population, can be a little harder to pin down. If you are a social media company, maybe your qualitative purpose is "to allow family and friends to stay connected." However, if your qualitative purpose does not fulfill your quantitative purpose, then you will not have the funds to remain in the game for an extended period of time. This misalignment led to the dot-com bust in the late 1990s, when many companies got hyper-focused on their qualitative purpose and forgot they had to make money.

Aligning Levels

The next level down from the organizational level, the group/team level, is where some get lost. Let's extend the social media company example above, and posit that advertising on your site is your main source of income. Your group is either supporting the sale of advertising or reducing the expense for generating this service. Accounts receivable's group-level purpose may be to facilitate a process that allows for quick and easy receipt of payments. Consumer IT's purpose may be to ensure that the platform has the ability to serve up as many advertising impressions as possible. Within IT there may be a website traffic team that has as its purpose generating as large a flow of user traffic as possible. Consumer marketing may work directly with traffic for the purpose of attracting a continuous inflow of users. This team's purpose aligns with the website traffic team, which aligns with the consumer IT purpose, which aligns with the overall systemic purpose. When purposes align, the groups function like members of a well-trained rowing team.

When I first joined a collegiate rowing team, I thought it was rather a waste of weight to have in the boat a person whose purpose was yelling at you to row. From the shores, I would hear, "Row, row, row," and think, "What the hell else are they going to do?" I mean they all had oars in their hands and they are sitting in a boat. It is not like they are going to have tea. That thought did not linger long in my mind when they set all eight of us out without a coxswain. Some rowed, others looked around, and one even started to look for music on his iPod. Even those rowing were not rowing in unison, so the boat started to go in squiggles and circles. The varsity team found it all amusing, as they doubled over in laughter watching from the dock.

We could all use a coxswain in our life reminding us of not only our purpose, but also keeping us in sync with the rest of the team. At the base level, we are all individual contributors. If we are not aligned at the individual contributor level, every level above will be skewed. Let's not confuse the individual contributor level with just those in the organization who do not manage people. Even people managers are individual contributors, (ICs).

Yes, people managers have greater influence because they lead a team of ICs, but they are, at the simplest form, just individuals who happen to contribute in a managerial capacity.

It is rather ironic that we have thousands of apps that will send us notifications and alerts all day long, distracting us from our purpose, but there is no app that helps us stay on the path toward our goals. It is the unawareness of purpose that impacts our work–life presence. What do I mean by that? If you do not understand the primary reason for doing something, it is easy for you to go off on unnecessary tangents, creating more stress and time loss. When you are stressed, your mind has a hard time being in the moment—in other words, being present. If you are someone who already finds it difficult to be mentally and physically co-located (meaning you are in one place physically, but mentally you are somewhere else), then stress will only exacerbate this issue.

Clarifying Your Purpose

In the Dagoba Group's leadership development workshop on achieving a healthy work–life balance, we have an activity we call "Clarifying Your Purpose." Just like the questioning path I explained earlier in this chapter, we start off with a simple question: What is the purpose of your organization, in one sentence? You may be surprised to find that many are unclear or are unable to communicate this in one sentence. After we complete that section of the workshop, we ask: What is the purpose of your job? This question is followed by a rather important alignment question: How does your job's purpose support your organizational purpose? At this point we see a lot of head scratching going on, though not as much as happens when we pose the next two questions.

First, what is your personal purpose? That question is designed to elicit an internal thought process that is rarely engaged. There are hundreds of books written on finding your purpose in life; some are probably a little closer to "finding meaning in life" than others. In this corporate context, your personal purpose is not meant to be an introspective analysis of the meaning of your existence. You can keep it as simple as you want: for example, why do you get up and go to work every day? Is it simply to make money, or are there other reasons? Some people's purpose is to provide for themselves and their families. In a previous job as a sales manager, I had conversations with my colleagues about our reasons for working. One sales rep's purpose was to put himself and his daughter through college. To keep that front of mind, I suggested he make a visual daily reminder. He cut out the front page of the brochure of both their preferred colleges. Each showed the name and a nice photo of the college campus. He then pinned the pages in his cubicle in front of his phone. This was why he came into work each day and picked up that phone. He went above and beyond the exercise, though. He got a duplicate set of pictures and placed them on his refrigerator at home, so they were front and center. This duplication of purpose at home allowed him to keep his work and personal life aligned, which brings us to the second question.

How does your job support your personal purpose? Although your current employment might not be your dream job, it can be in alignment with your personal purpose. You benefit most if you can discover how the place where you spend the majority of your waking hours supports your personal purpose. If you are working to provide for your family but your job keeps you away from your family for extended periods of time, causes you to continually miss important family events, or leaves you constantly distracted while at home, you may have a misalignment. Misalignment causes friction at home and in the office, and also encourages us not to be physically and mentally co-located.

When you are not co-located your ability to be fully present is disrupted, and so is your ability to be fully engaged, regardless of where you are. So what happens when you experience this lack of co-location? For this example, let's focus on the home side of the equation. A recent workshop attendee, Theresa, stayed after to thank us for the workshop and said that it gave her pause to think about what has been happening in her personal life and how that has impacted her professional standing. She sat down with me for coffee to tell me her story.

Theresa's Story

Theresa is a sales manager for a major pharmaceutical company. She is also a mother of three children and has been married for thirteen years to her husband, Hanover (she automatically explained that his name was given to him because of his place of birth). Her story is paraphrased below, and underlines a saying I have that "when you don't consciously choose your purpose, you default to possessions."

> I have always been someone who prided herself on being great at multitasking. As any parent knows, multitasking is a necessary skill set that is only amplified with each additional child. A month after the birth of my third child, you could find me at the kitchen table nursing the

newborn, using my foot to rock the two-year-old on his hobbyhorse, my left hand fiddling with building blocks with my five-year-old on the table, my right hand shopping on Amazon for diapers, all the while being on hold for another preschool interview. My husband and I called it "squiding." He was better at golf, but if you threw a few babies on that course, I could mop the floor with anyone. I became a sales manager two years before my first child. Hanover and I would stack our parental leave so each child had at least one parent home for the first four or five months.

Until this workshop, I never really thought about my personal purpose and how it related to work. I guess I was just in the default mode of making money and acquiring things. We were lucky enough to have salaries that would have allowed either one of us to leave their job and still support all the needs of the family. So the normal purpose of working primarily to support the family was not as prominent as it might be for others. I really didn't realize that not being clear on my purpose was an issue until I started to think about a number of recent experiences at work and home, and probably many more I forgot, that have been contributing to my stress levels. Since I was not very clear on my purpose, I realized I never thought about the purpose of my team.

I lost two reps in the past quarter. One told me she left for more money somewhere else. Two months later, I discovered through a mutual colleague that she had taken a job for the same salary, but told me it was for more money because that was what I would understand. The other one said his new job actually paid 25 percent less, but just seemed like more fun since it was at a small start-up with a highly social group. Although the two reps left for different reasons, they both felt unfulfilled, and my default goal of money was not resonating. So, on helping my reps discover how their personal purpose could be aligned with their job, I failed.

When the second rep quit, I came home in a bad mood. Every red light or slight delay ushered forth a moan or shout from me. It was Friday night, a time my husband and I reserved for going out sans children. At dinner, I was firing off e-mails to the recruiter and HR, as well as finishing up month-end reports while I was muttering, "Uh huh," to Hanover as he talked about his day with the children. "Theresa, put down the damn phone and be part of this conversation," he said, raising his voice in a way that attracted nearby diners' attention. Automatically, I retorted, "You sound just like my damn boss." Dinner was served just in time, and we ate in awkward silence.

Looking back on those instances and then doing this activity, everything seems to be clicking. All the while, I was thinking my work–life balance was seriously out of whack. The solution was simple: work from home more often and actually use my vacation time. However, that never seemed to do the trick. My stress levels would go down in the beginning but then spike back up. I always had an excuse about some temporary crisis or big client project or home problem. The list of excuses was endless. It was really not a balance issue, it was a presence issue. No matter where I was physically, I was not there mentally. When I was in a meeting with my boss, I was replying to texts and putting out fires via e-mail. There was probably not a single one-on-one with my staff when

I did not have to excuse myself to answer the phone or shoot off a quick e-mail. This behavior was replicated at home. My marriage had become stressed to the point that we were looking for a counselor. My kids resorted to screaming matches to capture my attention.

Although I need to flesh my ideas out more fully, the purpose exercise showed me how I was totally out of alignment in almost every way. Since I had not really considered my personal purpose, I just defaulted to acquiring things because that was easy; however, what I really valued were experiences. My job allowed me to not only have different experiences (travel, interactions with colleagues, team development), but also allowed me to afford more experiences with my family. I know I need to gain greater clarity on what type of experiences, but just getting to this level has really helped me. I can see how my job can be in alignment with my personal goals, but more importantly, I can mitigate the behavior that does not fit these goals. If I really want experiences with my children, I need to be there mentally for them. Just being physically near them does not count. The same for my husband. One of the actions that I wrote down for both sides of the work fence was to consciously state to myself and whomever I am with that "I am switching my phone to mute and putting it down for fifteen minutes." I figure I can add to that time, but I know my addiction needs to be taken one step at a time.

Discovering my own purpose will help me in helping my team uncover their purpose and better connect to their jobs and the company. It will also help us facilitate better one-on-ones and get one step closer to eliminating unnecessary distractions.

Consciously Choosing Your Purpose

Theresa participated in an action follow-up webinar sixty days after the workshop. We were discussing the actions participants had implemented and their overall impact. She mentioned her phone action (switching to mute and setting the phone aside for fifteen minutes), and said it was difficult to implement at first, as well as a bit awkward to say out loud that she was putting her phone down. She found putting it totally out of sight and reach worked better. Even fifteen-minute breaks from her phone improved her relationships at both home and work so much, because she was really listening to the person she was with. She even noticed that some of her reps were replicating her behavior after a very short period of time.

One other action she had identified was posting her personal, job, team, and company purpose. She posted them on the back of her office door so she saw them every time she went to hang up her coat, close the door for a meeting, or leave for the day. At home, she put her purpose on the inside door of a kitchen cabinet that held coffee cups so she was reminded every morning. Although she could not fully measure the effect, she said that, overall, she felt happier where she was, whether that was at home or at work, even though her work hours had not changed. She felt more balanced.

Many workshop participants come to realize that their family structure very much mimics their work structure. The family is the organization as a whole. The parents are executive leadership and the kids are individual contributors. Sometimes an older child takes on middle management duties. Work/chores are doled out according to the members' roles. This might be an odd way to look at the family unit, but it does come in handy when you are trying to create an overall alignment of goals. The family unit has a set of goals that lead down to teams and individual contributors. Workshop participants often come back to us and say they had a purpose conversation with the family as a whole, something they never even considered before.

Attaining greater presence at work undoubtedly contributes to greater presence at home and vice versa. This greater sense of presence does not stop at the front door of either the workplace or the home. Raising awareness of purpose at all levels will allow you to, first, notice you are out of alignment and, second, give you the ability to fix it.

When you do not consciously choose your purpose, you will most likely default to acquiring possessions. In a world where it seems everything is created to be obsolete as soon as you obtain it, there is always a bigger and better something; it is easy to get caught in the constant pursuit of possessions. Now, if you are making purchases as a conscious choice, then that is fine. The world needs consumers to keep our commercial engines running. It is not bad to turn to possessions even if you have another goal, such as educational experiences, for example. If you know that educational awareness is your purpose, then you can establish a filter for purchases. Perhaps a purchase of that Rosetta Stone Italian language package supports your overall purpose.

At work, a default to possessions means that you will focus excessively on compensation, often trading other, more enjoyable, aspects of your life for a greater payout. As a leader, it will give you a warped, one-sided sense of what motivates your team. As I noted in the previous chapter, PwC hit this factor square on when it realized its millennial recruits were not lured by the prospect of partnership as much as their baby boomer generation was. Had the company not created a greater sense of awareness at the systemic and team level, it would not have had this learning experience. With the employee population expected to be 80 percent millennials by 2020, a miss on this point could well spell disaster for the organization, especially if competitors got to the realization first.

Although it may seem to some a bit foreign to speak of purpose at all levels, it is a very useful activity that pays bottom-line results. One of those results is the ability for everyone to reevaluate her distractions—these could be as simple as gratuitous e-mails, unnecessary meetings, or endless committee work. As a leader, being aware of your purpose at each level will help you personally, but more importantly it will help your team all row in the same direction at the same time. It is the first step to achieving a healthy work–life balance.

Discussion Points

- What is your organizational purpose? What is your job's purpose?
- How does your job support the organizational purpose?
- What is your personal purpose and how does work support this purpose?
- Are all purpose levels aligned?

Takeaways

- ✓ Purpose can and should be found at all levels.
- ✓ The quantitative purpose fuels the shareholder engine, while the qualitative purpose fuels the employee engine.
- ✓ Alignment of purpose will allow for the elimination of nonessential distractions.

- ✓ Behavior at work will likely mimic behavior at home, and vice versa.
- ✓ Staying in alignment takes practice and constant vigilance.
- ✓ We could all use a coxswain in our lives, not only to remind us of our purpose but also to keep us in sync with the rest of the team.

Chapter 4

Achieving Balance and Presence in Work

Work is not a four-letter word.

When an organization starts to rally around the work–life balance topic, its first impulse is to implement quick systemic fixes such as reduced hours, mandatory vacations, or work-from-home policies. Although these policies, if leveraged in the right way, can be helpful, they are not effective in and of themselves. Work is often viewed as the culprit when employees suffer from a work–life imbalance, and it is sometimes referred to in the same tone of voice people use for four-letter words: "Ugh, I have to go to *work* tomorrow." This statement is usually followed by a sigh and a little bit of empathy from friends. Emphasis on the "little bit," because almost everyone has to go to work at some point. Misery does love company.

However, work does not and should not be a four-letter word. It's true that some of us have difficult jobs. And yes, we are not all in our dream jobs. If we are able to align work with our personal purpose as discussed in the previous chapter, however, work can be far more fulfilling. What can we do as individuals, leaders, and organizations to create a healthier balance in and out of work?

Fixing Time

There are three core categories ripe for change: *fixing time, practicing presence,* and *setting boundaries.* Because imbalance is historically seen as a time issue, the first silo I will explore is fixing time. The word "fixing" is used deliberately because many believe it is somehow broken—or at least that the process by which we dole time out to ourselves or others is malfunctioning.

Work-from-Home Policies

In this chapter, I will focus on the traditional knee-jerk policies mentioned previously, as well as on some more practical and immediately implementable actions that can be taken at the individual level. Let's work on what some believe is the biggest fixer of time, the now somewhat controversial policy that permits individuals to work from home. First, why do we, either as individuals or organizations, believe a work-from-home policy will help create a healthier work–life balance? Because the general populace perceives the work–life issue to be a problem of too much time at work, a policy that allows people to be at home more naturally seems like a simple solution.

If you take a deeper dive, there are some reasons that a work-from-home policy could provide greater benefit. The U.S. Census Bureau 2009 American Community Survey found that the average commuting time for someone working in the United States was a little more than twenty-five minutes, one way. As anyone who lives in a metropolitan area would agree, less than half an hour would be a dream commute. Many in metro areas face trips that are one hour or longer each way. At one time, I was working in southern New Jersey and commuting to north central Jersey, for a round trip of approximately three hours each day. A work-from-home policy theoretically gives an employee these three hours back each day, to devote to either work or personal life, or simply to allow something close to the suggested healthy amount of sleep time. In my opinion, this commuter dividend is one of the strongest arguments for work-from-home policies. There are other tangential arguments that come from the commuter dividend, including that it is a more environmentally friendly option, it increases safety (from reduced auto accidents), and it results in overall lower transportation expenses.

However, the logic of this argument rests on the idea that you will redirect the time you save to more productive tasks, and therein lies the difficulty. If you do not develop an awareness of purpose and create a work–life strategy, there is a good chance that any time you save by not commuting will dissipate in some other time vacuum. Maybe you know you can sleep in so you watch TV later at night. Instead of taking that found time for exercise, you spend it on work e-mails. Lucky you, you get to answer e-mails even earlier in the morning! Only you know your own personal time wasters, so you can fill in the blank when asked what you would end up doing with your saved commute time.

The work-from-home option has been pulled off the policy shelves at many organizations, most notably Yahoo, which created a lot of discussion when it began restricting work-at-home options. The policy wasn't discontinued because organizations discovered another solution to the work–life balance issue, but rather because they did not see the expected payoff. Let's face it, it is tough to be focused on work when you are at home. A few individuals handle it quite well, while the majority finds it difficult or nearly impossible. The 2007 Economist Intelligence Unit "Business in Motion, Managing the Mobile Workforce" report sponsored by Alcatel-Lucent found "Internationally, 68 percent of teleworkers say that the blurring of the boundaries between work and home life is the biggest downside to working at home."

For those trying to create a healthier balance, these blurred boundaries can have an impact opposite of the one intended: rather than spending more time on home life, you might let office tasks bleed into home time because work is always present. It is far too easy to slip into work mode if you can't sleep, get up early, feel a little bored, or just have to check one more time if that report came in. Easy access means the potential for distraction.

On the flip side, companies found that personal surroundings provided an increased distraction for employees, preventing them from being truly focused on the work task at hand. How many of us have been on conference calls with someone working from home who had a dog barking, children screaming, a doorbell ringing, or even the TV on in the background? Entire industries have sprung up around creating work space and practices to help separate the two spheres. If neither you nor the company is achieving greater balance, then all the other liabilities around this policy pile up quickly. Companies report less spontaneous innovation, weaker peer relationships, and more challenging communication.

Can a work-from-home policy generate a healthier work–life balance? The answer is a resounding yes, but with a few caveats. Employees need to be trained on creating boundaries and achieving physical–mental colocation. Leaders need to agree on and respect those boundaries. Leaders who offer work-from-home opportunities are encouraged to create an agreement that outlines what is and is not acceptable. The agreement does not have to go into minute detail, as the roommate agreement featured in the hit TV series *The Big Bang Theory* does, but it needs to include some basics. The policy should benefit the employee as much as it does the employer. Ideally, a work-from-home agreement should contain the following:

1. Work hours—When is the employee expected to be working and accessible to colleagues? When is it considered inappropriate for workmates to contact the employee for nonemergency situations? What defines an emergency situation?

2. Communication—What are acceptable modes of communication (e.g., instant chat, e-mail, phone call, Skype, etc.)? Will the employee keep these available during all work hours?

3. Face time—Not to be confused with the Apple video application—I am talking about actual human contact. What is the expected amount of time the employee should be in the office on a weekly or monthly basis? Does the employee attend group meetings in person? Is he invited and/or expected to attend social events?

4. Attire—Although a dress code may seem silly when you think about working from home, if you are doing any type of video conferencing, include an agreement about attire that conforms to the acceptable office dress policy. Work clothes also help employees and their families create boundaries around when work has begun and ended.

5. Work space—A Herman Miller research project discovered that 48 percent of people work from their bedroom. A separate work space, whenever possible, definitely helps to create boundaries. Does the employer invest in work space creation?

Work-from-home employees and their leaders should also be given mandatory development on how to best leverage this opportunity and when to question its viability. Sometimes it is the work-from-home employee who is very effective with the policy, but her undeveloped manager has difficulty leading remotely. The setup has to work for both the employee and the manager if the organization is to realize full benefits. The policy needs to be implemented systemically, rather than on a manager-by-manager basis. When it is rolled out on a one-off basis, there is potential for an inequitable impact on particular employee groups. For example, a manager may have an unconscious bias; he might believe some groups of people are hard workers who do not need an office structure, while other groups need more supervision and thus need to work in the office. This can happen along many dimensions of difference. Generations is an easy example. Perhaps the manager views older employees more favorably to work from home than younger generations. It is far too easy for managers to make "special exceptions" for certain employees due to their relationship while excluding everyone else from having the same opportunity.

Mandatory Vacation

One solution that needs to be rolled out on a system-wide basis is a more liberal vacation policy. Reworking the vacation policy, often to require employees to take time off, is a common approach to creating a healthier work–life balance. Let's take the same lens to this approach that I did with the work-from-home policy. First, why would one think mandatory vacation is a good solution to difficulties with work–life balance?

As I noted earlier, when work–life balance comes up as a topic within an organization, the conversation often flows to employees not having enough time in their personal lives. Requiring vacations is a logical step that would allow employees more non-work time. According to the Bureau of Labor Statistics, three-quarters of the U.S. working population is allocated paid time off as a work benefit. The time allocated and the percentage of the working population receiving this benefit is much higher in other countries. The key word in that sentence is "allocated," because it is not always taken. A 2014 Robert Half *Vacation Days: Are You a Saver or a Spender* survey found that two out of five employees do not use all of their paid vacation leave. The 2009 *Daily News* article "Amidst Recession Pressures Most Workers Didn't Use All of Their Vacation Days" noted a 2009 Right Management survey that found 66 percent of employees did not use all of their vacation days. Regardless of the survey results, there are millions of workers who do not use their vacation time. The article went on to note Right Management's CEO Douglas Matthews who said, "Not taking a vacation can backfire on companies because it causes stress and other health issues that lower productivity."

There are varying reasons for the phenomenon in which employees neglect to take the paid time off their company provides them. In some cases, an employee is saving up for a big event, while others find they just cannot fit vacation into their work schedule. In the introduction, I wrote about a former employer that offered unlimited vacation time for sales staff, though I soon discovered that the unwritten norm was not to take vacation or risk a frown from management, together with all that comes with the frown.

So if an organization is seeing a bank of vacation days build up among its employees, even as it notes an increasing stress point around work–life balance, encouraging employees to use up those days seems to be a good idea. The challenge lies in the details and the perception and the legality. How does a company roll out a policy that encourages or requires employees to use vacation time and is in compliance with local laws? The answer: carefully.

There are a couple of popular choices an organization may make: a "use it or lose it" policy or mandatory time off. The "use it or lose it" policy is not legal in every jurisdiction. For example, in California a "use it or lose it" vacation policy is illegal. However, it is important to note that California does not require a company to provide a paid or unpaid vacation benefit. In order to be an employer of choice, however, most companies do offer paid vacation time.

Even if it is legal in your jurisdiction, a "use it or lose it" policy can be perceived as a benefit to the company, because the organization can avoid allowing any employee to build up a bank of time that will potentially need to be paid out should the employee leave. The term "use it or lose it" also seems to exacerbate the whole stress factor around work–life balance. When an employee believes she cannot take vacation because of a disapproving manager or because she feels her workload is too heavy to allow time off, then the "lose it" part seems like additional punishment.

Mandatory policies that simply require vacation time be used can also be perceived as a backhand rather than a helping hand. Sun Microsystems, HP, and Motorola have all used this policy in varying degrees. Manufacturing is most known for this policy, as most manufacturers close during down periods, and some require employees to use their vacation time for these breaks in production. In this sense, it is seen more as a company savings rather than as a tool to improve the lives of employees.

Mandatory or "use it or lose it" policies do encourage increased use of vacation time, but they need to be implemented strategically if the goal is to assuage a work–life imbalance. Following is a quick example that shows how either of these policies may provide zero impact to the work–life balance situation. Sharon's employer instituted a "use it or lose it" policy to help stem the growing burnout rate at the company. Sharon's boss, not wanting her to lose vacation time, required her to take time off before the end of the year.

Sharon could not envision keeping up with her workload as an accounts payable manager if she took a whole week or more off at a time, so she decided to take off every Friday for three months. Neither Sharon nor her manager had received any type of training or guidance on this work–life-balance-induced policy other than a suggestion to spend more time at home. Sharon worked later on Thursdays because she knew she would not be in on Friday. Like clockwork, though, she started e-mailing her team at the start of the day on Friday. She would get caught up in one crisis or deadline or another, and ended up working the whole day. Her boss initially chided Sharon for working on her day off, but gave up after a couple of failed attempts to get her to stop. By the end of the three months, Sharon not only worked every Friday from home, but spent more hours in the office every Thursday evening. The net difference was a loss of personal time. With her behavior, Sharon also created an unwritten expectation for her team that they should work while on vacation. This was not the impact the company had originally intended.

So how can this policy be managed for the proper impact? First, be aware of the difference between work–life presence and work–life balance. All too often, employees perceive work–life balance as simply a good distribution of hours in terms of physical location. If the organization does not promote a culture in which employees are expected to be mentally and physically co-located, then no amount of vacation time rigging will make a serious impact. Work–life presence is all about this co-location. When you are at home physically, you should attempt to be there mentally as well. The same goes for the time you spend at work physically; you should be at work mentally, too.

Second, a vacation policy geared toward reducing employee burnout and allowing for mental refreshing should come with a more thought-out strategy than a simple suggestion to employees that they take time off. If the organization believes time off for employees is vital to its continued success with its talent and its standing in the marketplace, then it should provide development to encourage the appropriate behavior. At the very least, there should be a general understanding of what work the employee is expected to do or not to do when she is on vacation. The agreement could be complex, or it could be as simple as the paragraph below:

> I, [INSERT NAME], will use my vacation time to disconnect from work, which means I will not access e-mail or spend time on any work projects. My manager, [INSERT NAME], understands and approves that I will not be checking e-mail or spending time on work projects. The only exception, if any, will be [INSERT PROJECT], which will be managed on [NAME DAY] between [START TIME] and [END TIME].

As leaders, we do need to understand that every policy needs flexibility. There are times when a project cannot be turned off, unfortunately. Perhaps you currently lean on techs to maintain your Oracle servers and you cannot afford for the servers to be down, but at the same time you don't want to burn out your current resource. Or maybe there is a large client RFP with a looming deadline. The exception clause allows the employee and the boss to create a release valve, so both can feel good about the time the employee turns off. If there is no critical need like the one just noted, this piece of the clause should be deleted.

Before an organization fiddles with its vacation policy to generate more use, HR executives, company leaders, and others involved should discuss why the buildup of days is a liability beyond the potential payout issue. How does an imbalance between work and life show up in the organization and on the bottom line? Ask leaders why employees are not using their time, and provide them some guidance on how to pass down this development to their team. If development is done well and employees are genuinely encouraged to take time to disconnect and recharge, mandatory vacation policy may never need to be implemented, yet a highly beneficial impact on employee work–life balance would accrue.

Reduced Hours

Much like discussions about the vacation policy issue, those about reducing work hours can fall into the trap of providing more physical time out of the office, but the mental time attached to work has not decreased. My first job out of college was with the world's largest nonprofit membership organization, AARP. Early on, the organization set a thirty-five-hour workweek. Although this schedule helped to tip the scales toward non-work time, there were plenty of individuals who continued to feel burned out. It bears repeating that organizations that do not provide development and guidance for systemic work–life balance policy changes are unlikely to fully capture the intended goals.

How many hours cut from the workweek would make a difference? Are the hours really just cut on paper, with employees feeling that they are still expected to work the full schedule? Even if you could offer fewer hours, some employees may not want such a schedule if it comes with reduced compensation and/or benefits. Once hours move an employee from full time to part time, the employee may not qualify with the company for health insurance and retirement savings benefits. How does the company compensate for those lost hours? Is it possible or logical to hire more staff to cover the lost work time?

Just as the work-from-home policy may not be culturally appropriate to offer, reduced work hours may not be within the leader's toolbox due to budgetary or workload constraints. Like the first two policy changes discussed in this section, reduced hours may well be a systemic change that is outside a leader's area of influence. If you want to make a difference but are restrained by systemic challenges, there are still many practical actions that you, as a leader, can implement independently. These would, of course, work better when done in concert with teams focusing on this topic at an organizational level.

The Fifty-Minute Meeting

This is the easiest and quickest change you as a leader can take on right now. If you are using a calendar function such as Outlook, you will notice that it defaults to one-hour increments. It is so easy to schedule back-to-back meetings. Your 9 a.m. meeting ends at 10 a.m., sending you running off for your 10 a.m. meeting, and so on for the remainder of the day. Each meeting entails notes that need to be digested, together with a list of to-dos. However, since you are scheduled back to back, none of these items gets done unless you either (1) work during lunch—and then you can only tackle the morning meeting tasks—or (2) attack them at the end of the day, keeping you in the office for another two hours. Perhaps, like many of us, you eventually take this work home. Coupled with all these meetings are endless e-mail cascades that can keep you busy from morning to night reading and responding, creating what some refer to as e-mail addiction.

Do you or somebody you know continually check for e-mail and then respond at any waking moment? This reinforcing behavior mimics the social media post-and-check-for-response addiction. Way before the Internet was even a glimmer of a thought, Ivan Pavlov demonstrated how classical conditioning could be used with dogs by ringing a bell before they were given something to eat. When the process was repeated enough times, the dog would salivate the moment a bell was rung. Now, think quickly. What happens when your phone rings to signify you got a text message or an e-mail? Every time you get an e-mail or a social media response, your brain gives you a tiny treat of dopamine. If you check and are rewarded enough times, you will slowly condition yourself into needless time-wasting behavior that forces you to be mentally and physically dislocated. Pavlov would be fascinated to see how we are now the trained dogs and the bell being rung is carried willingly in our pockets.

Classical conditioning can also work in your favor. Have you ever been to a meeting scheduled for one hour that cannot be accomplished in fifty minutes? In my twenty-five years of work experience, I cannot think of a single meeting that would have been seriously impacted by shaving ten minutes off. It does take some conditioning to think of fifty or twenty minutes past the hour (whether you started at the top or middle of the hour) as end points. It is easy to do in your calendar function by simply typing in the time. If you have a tech guru, perhaps ask that person to fix the default to fifty-minute meetings instead of the sixty-minute system setting. The hard part will come when you are leading meetings—you have to train your mind to truly perceive the end to be ten minutes earlier. One-hour meetings are simply habit, and have no logical reasoning behind them other than that they are a social norm.

Pavlov's dog got treats and e-mail addicts get dopamine, so what does the fifty-minute meeting provide to reinforce that behavior? Well, naturally you get ten minutes, but it is what you do with those ten minutes that makes the difference. You could step outside to breathe fresh air, use the restroom, digest the notes, grab a bite to eat, do one meeting task, stretch, walk, or even take a mindful minute (more on this later). If you did this for five meetings a day, you just gave yourself back almost an hour of time. After a week, you realized more than half a day of reclaimed time. What could you do with an additional half day of time during the workweek?

For half-hour meetings, change the time span to twenty-five minutes. Institute a policy of your team of never having thirty- or sixty-minute meetings. Or, if you are in a company that has a culture of never being on time because attendees are running from other meetings that end at the top of the hour, consider starting your meetings at ten minutes or a quarter past the hour. These changes will take repeated behavioral enforcement. Remember that it was career-long classical conditioning that had you and your team scheduling hour-long meetings regardless of how much time you really needed, so it will take some time to get out of this habit. You will be surprised by how this little change impacts the overall attitude and demeanor of the office.

Flex Start and End Time

Can a flexible start and end time provide inclusion value? Employees who are also caregivers (either for their children or for their parents) can be bound by inflexible day care start and end hours. Commuters may find they can shave an hour or more from their daily commute by beating rush hour in either direction. Those who rely on public transportation may be limited in their ability to meet standard office hours. An employee's ability to move her workday time forward or backward an hour may be hugely helpful in reducing personal life stress. Not all employers can offer this option because they may be tied to external systemic forces such as brokers and the opening or closing of the stock market. Such flex times may also mean that traditional meeting times need to be changed. As a leader, you should explore the possibility with your team, decide whether flex start and end time is feasible, and, if it is, set expectations. Expectations may concern the amount of flex time allowed (such as one hour), advance notice needed, or times when it is not allowed. Could an employee work two hours in the morning from home and then commute into work to finish her work hours? Or do the same in the afternoon so he is there when his child arrives home from school? Speak with your team to determine if this is a viable option and what would be the best way to implement for the benefit of the entire team.

Practicing Presence

Fixing your time so you are more efficient allows you to spend more energy on being present. What good is all that extra time if you are still not able to be mentally and physically co-located?

Following are a few ideas you can develop to be more present in or out of work.

Mindful Minutes

As I mentioned, the minutes reclaimed by cutting meeting times could be spent in so many ways. As my father would say when he dispersed our allowances, "You don't need to spend it all in one place." Those extra ten minutes do not need to be spent in any particular way to be effective, but there is one practice you might do each time you find yourself with an extra ten minutes that you may find surprisingly refreshing—a mindful minute. What is that? The mindful minute is more about what it isn't than what it is: it is about giving yourself sixty seconds of nothingness. It is not meditation, although it can certainly move in that direction if you choose. It is simply a respite for your mind. You do not need to practice any special chant or philosophy. You do not need to clear your mind. You do not need to focus on your breathing, though that does help.

Try it for yourself. Go somewhere where you will not be bothered. If you have an open office environment, that might be difficult. Some have told us that they have found the bathroom stall to be the only place where they can get any alone time in the office. If that is your situation, then so be it. Use what works for you. Set a time on your smartphone, watch, or other device for sixty seconds. When you press start, just close your eyes. If you are instructed to clear your mind, you may find it troubling that so many thoughts keep slipping in, so don't worry about doing that. It is best if you try to focus on one thing internally, such as your heartbeat or breathing. Breathe deeply and slowly, holding each breath for a second or two longer than you normally would. Your timing device allows you to forget about trying to determine whether a minute has gone by or not.

Before reading on, go ahead and do it. Don't worry; the book will be here when you get back.

Did you do it? What did it feel like? If you have never done this before, you may be amazed at how long a minute feels when you are constantly bombarded with stimuli. We try this exercise in our workshop, but do not tell them it will be for a minute. At the end of the exercise, typically more than half the participants swear the time period was far longer than a minute. I had a chance to listen to a participant explain the exercise to a colleague who did not attend the workshop. His colleague just raised his eyebrows and said a minute was nothing and he could do anything for a minute. So his colleague challenged him to hold his breath for a minute. Not to be outdone, he tried, but only lasted about forty-five seconds.

The whole purpose of this exercise is to condition yourself to interrupt the ceaseless movement of work life. Remember the laws of inertia: a body in motion tends to stay in motion. If you can spend more time than a minute then great, but sixty seconds is enough to put on the brakes without disrupting the needs of the day. It is hard to regain balance when you are constantly falling forward. If you feel comfortable trying this with your team, do it at the beginning of a meeting. You could simply say you are going to have a moment of silence. Other than instructing them to put any e-devices on silent and out of reach, there is no need to be prescriptive, such as telling them to close their eyes or focus on their breathing. Allow them to pass the minute in their own fashion. It may feel a bit awkward at first, but do this often enough and you will find your team actually asking for it. Some of us already do this at home, when we have a silent moment of prayer before a meal or quietly wait for the coffee to percolate, or while we are absentmindedly petting our dog or cat.

A Quiet Space

Those who try to practice a mindful minute may uncover a need in the office: a place for disconnection. In the heyday of dot-coms, there was a fad of setting aside a room where those seeking downtime could escape. As offices got crowded and budgets got crunched, this room, as well as many a conference room, was converted into an office. I would encourage you, as a leader, to take inventory of your space to see if there is a way to reclaim a private quiet space. It could be a large supply closet or a rarely used conference room. Increasingly, airports offer small private rooms—the planners can configure ten rooms from even a small space. Each room basically offers passengers the ability to shut out the rest of the world for the short period between flights.

Quiet rooms can be used for myriad reasons, and provide additional value to your team. Some may use the room for ritual prayers, while others may find it handy for taking care of certain personal or medical tasks they'd rather not do in the restroom. One woman told me that her last employer had such a room, and she found it extremely useful as a lactation room, as she perceived the restroom to be unsanitary. Another said he did not like taking his insulin shots in the bathroom for the same reason, and was happy to have a private place outside of the cubical pit to administer them.

The inclusive value of instituting a quiet room reminds me

of the initial debate of making building entrances accessible to those with disabilities. For the most part, legislation had to be enacted before buildings would make the necessary renovations. Today, there are more people using that ramp than the ones it was originally designed for. Delivery drivers, people with suitcases, parents with children in tow, and many others find the front-door ramp to be extremely useful. Although I will go into the inclusive aspect of creating a balanced work–life culture in a later chapter, as leaders we should continually take a holistic look at any policy or practice from an inclusive lens to see if it would provide a diversity of solutions.

Setting Boundaries

Much of establishing a work–personal life balance is about setting boundaries, such as what is and isn't acceptable in a flexible start program or the use of quiet rooms (e.g., no sleeping or playing video games). Boundaries can be physical or mental.

For example, one physical boundary you might set is: no social media posting or personal texting while at your desk. If you need to do those things, force yourself to go to the kitchen or outside. This practice will help you and your team be more focused on the task at hand. It is also an example of the flexibility of boundaries. There are times when we need to take care of personal business during the workday. Give yourself and the team the ability to do that while also separating personal tasks from the primary work space. Boundaries that do not have some margin of built-in flexibility usually don't last.

Mental boundaries tend to revolve around helping people

be mentally and physically co-located. A mental boundary might be not looking at your e-device when you are in conversation with someone or in a meeting. I would suggest that those who have e-device addictions start off slowly by saying they will only allow themselves to look at their devices once every five minutes and then expand that time up to thirty minutes.

In the next chapter, I will focus on how boundaries in your personal life can be relationship savers, but in this chapter I will focus on workplace relationships. Nothing says to your direct reports that they are not important more than your inability to set aside all things digital. If there are already some inclusion challenges in the office, your inability to be mentally and physically co-located when someone different from you is in the office may exacerbate those issues. For example, if gender inequality is perceived to be a factor in your office, not paying full attention to women when they are in one-on-ones with you may be seen as another example of this inequality. Everyone loves to receive full attention; I call it the Bill Clinton effect. I continually hear that, regardless of your political leanings, when President Clinton is speaking to you, you feel like you are the only person in the room. When was the last time you saw a successful politician continually checking his mobile device while he was engaging people?

Think about the times you engage your colleagues and reports; one-on-ones, meetings, mealtime, or at social events. Now make a list of distractions that may draw your attention away from them during those times. If you have a trusted colleague or assistant, ask that person to write down things he believes take your focus away. Disrupt that tendency by setting boundaries around those distractions.

Boundaries only work if you:

1. Increase awareness of what creates needless distractions.
2. Develop ways to mitigate those distractions.
3. Communicate these boundaries to your team and management.
4. Maintain these boundaries at least 90 percent of the time.

It is understandable that emergencies arise and boundaries need to be crossed, but those occurrences should add up to less than 10 percent of the time. If you find that limit constantly exceeded, you will need to reassess the situation and potentially develop new boundaries.

A three-pronged approach to fix time, practice presence, and set boundaries will help you and your team foster a healthier balance between work and personal life. The ideas in this chapter are just starters to get you to think more creatively about the practical things you can do to make a difference. Move toward a happier situation in the office and then focus your attention at home. In the next chapter I will take a more individual approach to personal life, so you can mirror your success at fostering balance in work.

Discussion Points

- What is the impact on your organization when attention is not given to work–life balance?
- Has your organization announced a work–life balance policy with great intention that did not live up to its goals? Why?

- Which of the three core changes (i.e., fixing time, practicing presence, setting boundaries) would you find most beneficial? Could you implement one of them immediately?

Takeaways

✓ There are three core areas of change that help organizations improve work–life balance: fixing time, practicing presence, and setting boundaries.

✓ Work–life policies without leadership development often fail.

✓ Both a remote manager and a work-from-home employee need to set expectations for a successful working relationship.

✓ When boundaries get blurred, work and personal life are more likely to be off balance.

Chapter 5

Achieving a Personal Life Balance

Expect to fall. Plan to get up.

Some may find it surprising that achieving balance in your work life can be much easier than achieving it in your personal life, which is one of the reasons I focus on work life first. For the most part, work is structured and operates under a fairly consistent system. There are written rules of order and generally accepted norms.

When it comes to personal life, you can throw all of that out the window. Very rarely do you find (nor do most people want to find) a home structure with thought-out written policies. You most likely do not have a team in one of your guest bedrooms constantly trying to optimize and improve the well-being of the family organization. Nor are you likely to have a family handbook that helps guide your daily interactions. You will, however, have unwritten norms, traditions, and an expected range of behavior. Without the support you have in the corporate culture, it is easier for behaviors in the personal arena to slowly shift into unhealthy norms.

In a corporation, there is typically a shared goal at the group/team level that aligns with the goal of the organization. We spoke about aligning purpose in chapter 3. Part of creating that alignment is determining your personal purpose for devoting thirty to fifty years to getting up every morning and investing your energy in an organization. Spending some time to really understand and write down not only why you go to work but why you go to this particular job will help you create alignment, letting you find greater balance at work while also providing a firm foundation for your personal life.

In the previous chapter, I spoke to the three core change categories for achieving presence and balance in work as being: fixing time, practicing presence, and setting boundaries. Although those silos can carry over to your personal life, we perceive them a bit differently at home. In your personal life, the core challenges are in one of the following three m's: *managing priorities, mitigating addictions,* and *minding now.*

Managing Priorities

Life, especially home life, is a fine act of juggling many priorities. For every person you provide care to, whether a child or an adult, you add ten more balls to that juggling act. Most working adults have only four to five hours of waking time at home during the weekdays, so it is no wonder that it is easier to maintain balance with regard to work than to personal life.

There is a fairly easy awareness activity that can help you become more attuned to all your competing priorities. Ready? Get out a blank sheet of paper. Do not do this exercise on the computer—there are far too many alerts and triggers on the computer that will pull your attention away. First things first, write your personal purpose at the top of the page. If you do not know your purpose yet, just write down what you would like it to be. Beneath your purpose, draw two vertical lines from the top of the page to the bottom, so you have three columns. Write "Time Demands" as the first column heading, "My Investment" as the second column heading, and "Priority" as the third column heading.

In the left-hand column, start listing everything in your personal life that demands your time at home. Don't add any work-related activities just yet. Typically, home demands can be bucketed into the things we have to do, but do not like, such as chores (laundry, cleaning, shopping, cooking, yard care); things we would prefer to do all day, like hobbies (music, video games, painting, exercise, reading, watching TV); and time with our loved ones, including family obligations (to spouse, children, parents, pets). You do not have to group them, but it does help you understand how you perceive each time demand. For example, some of us may perceive yard care as a chore, while those who enjoy it would categorize it as a hobby. Dropping off and picking up little Bobby at soccer practice may be seen either as a chore or family obligation. Exercise is usually a toss-up between a chore and a hobby for most of us. There is no right or wrong answer; the category you choose will depend upon how you perceive the activity.

In the middle column, write down the amount of time you believe you spend doing that particular activity in the course of a week. Try to average the time across weeks: if it takes you two hours to shuttle Bobby to soccer practice each week but you only do two weeks a month, then average the time by writing down one hour a week. When you write down the hours estimated, total your time at the bottom of the sheet. This is your perceived time demand. We often overestimate the time it takes to complete chores while underestimating the time we spend on hobbies. You will have a chance to create a more accurate time-table later. This activity is a quick and dirty awareness checker.

Now, in the third column write a number from one to five beside each time demand. One designates "must do to avoid seri-ous consequences" (e.g., lack of exercise can lead to ill health). Three is "nice to have." Five is "can easily miss without any con-sequences" (e.g., not playing Angry Birds). Two and four are the in-betweens. Don't overthink your answers, just jot down the number that first comes to mind for each task.

Now circle all of the number ones and put a line through all of the number fives. This is your first step to managing your pri-orities at home. There are a few more steps to this process, but you can post this page on the fridge or in another visible place for now. When you are ready, take on the next two steps, which may take a little longer.

On another sheet of paper, write your work purpose at the top. Draw two vertical lines to create three columns, like you just did on the first sheet. Write "Time Demands," "My Invest-ment," and "Priority" at the top of each successive column. Now write all the things you do for work when you are not on the clock (meaning, the time you are supposed to be spending doing all the things on the first list). If you are like most people, reading/responding to e-mails will be at the top of your list. Research, reports, meetings, or phone calls may also populate your list. Again, estimate the amount of time you spend per week, on average, for each task, and then give each a priority level between one and five, with one as the highest priority and five as the lowest. Remember, this is time you spend on work activities outside normal work hours. It is time for you to be honest about each item in terms of its priority. If you waited to read e-mails until first thing the next morning when you got to work, would there really be any major consequences? Could you do that company research when you are at work? Does that work call have to be answered at 8 p.m.?

The last step of this awareness activity will take a little more time. It is a step that often surprises many who take it on. It is about tracking reality. Make a copy of both your lists (the personal and the work list) and carry them with you for the next couple of weeks. Every time you engage in one of the activities on your list, write down the start and stop time. If you are a big user of a smartphone, you can use it to track your time. Every phone call and text chain will have a time duration stamp. Note even the small blips of time. For example, include the two minutes you spent looking at e-mail while at lunch or the ten minutes in line at Starbucks, which are not on your list. The goal is to get a realistic inventory of the time you are truly investing.

Once you are aware of time sinks, such as the two hours you spent watching TV reruns, you will be able to better prioritize your limited time for home life; you'll not only see ways to decrease those time wasters, but also ways to increase the time you spend on activities that provide you greater value and joy. Focus on ensuring the number-one priorities are fulfilled, and then pick and choose those tasks that have lower priority but greater fulfillment. Over time, you may find the number ones really are threes or fours. And if you gave an activity like reading a number five, you may realize that there is a consequence to your happiness when you skip these fulfilling activities, so you might want to rate that item higher.

Since I just broached the subject of happiness, this is a good time to touch on the subject. A healthy life balance is usually conflated with greater happiness. They can definitely go hand in hand, but you can have balance and not happiness. The reverse is typically not true, however. When your life is out of balance, your stress increases, you are deprived of sleep, and your nerves get short, all foes of happiness. This book is not about achieving happiness, though I often see it as a side benefit. After you achieve greater balance, I suggest that you read one of my favorite books on the subject, *Happiness at Home,* by Gretchen Rubin. Rubin is an expert in the field of the pursuit of happiness. We employ many of her tips/rules at our home. Rubin speaks to changing habits or, in some cases our addictions, which is a nice segue to our second *m.*

Mitigating Addictions

Society often connects the word *addictions* with drug or alcohol abuse, or another practice that may be detrimental to our health. In this book, when I speak of addictions, I am talking about time addictions: those activities that provide little value, easily absorb inordinate amounts of time, and take us away from the people we love. Following is a partial list of common time addictions:

- E-mail—A 2012 *Daily Mail* article stated that an average office worker spends 2.5 hours every day (or the equivalent of eighty-one workdays a year) reading and responding to e-mails.
- Video games—According to the 2014 Nielsen *360° Gaming Report,* a U.S. gamer thirteen or older spends more than six hours a week playing video games.
- Texting—A 2014 Baylor University study published in the *Journal of Behavioral Addictions* found that we are spending, on average, ninety-four minutes a day texting. James Roberts of Baylor University and Stephen Pirog of Seton Hall University also noted in their *Journal of Behavioral Addictions* study that young adults are sending out 3,200 texts per month.

- Social media—A GlobalWebIndex 2015 *QTR1 Social Media Engagement* study of 170,000 users found that we are spending close to two hours a day on social media such as Facebook, Twitter, and LinkedIn. The same study found the average user has 5.5 accounts and is active on three platforms. Furthermore, Facebook has half of their users visiting the platform multiple times a day.
- Photography (from selfies to every meal)—A 2015 OnePoll online poll in the U.K. found young women are spending up to forty-eight minutes per day taking photos, most of which are selfies, to post to online sites such as Instagram and Facebook. That is more than five hours per week just taking and posting selfies!
- TV—The Nielson March 2014 *Cross-Platform Report* found Americans spend close to five hours a day watching TV.
- YouTube—According to the January 2016 *DMR YouTube Statistic Report,* more than four billion videos are viewed per day, accumulating to over six billion hours of video per month.
- Video streaming services such as Netflix, Hulu, and Amazon Prime—According to the 2014 Nielsen *Total Audience Report*, we spend fifty minutes more time per day when the household has access to subscription video-on-demand services.

If you are a numbers person like me, you may be adding up the above numbers in disbelief. The amount of time spent on just the above adds up to far more than there are waking hours at home. There are a couple of reasons for this mismatch of time spent and time available. First, the studies do not differentiate between activities that are done at home and at work. ComScore's *Total Video* report actually noted that the peak time for watching TV online is during the workday. Second, it is becoming increasingly common to "multitask" in time-wasting activities. TV is just the gateway drug to time wasting. The same ComScore five-week study showed that 61 percent of us are watching TV and surfing online concurrently. As a matter of fact, if we watch TV online, then our actual time spent watching TV increases by 25 percent!

There is debate today in academia and the medical field on the addiction level of activities such as e-mail checking, TV watching, and Internet surfing. The Baylor University study noted above had 60 percent of its survey respondents admit that they believe they are addicted to these activities. The same study found women are glued to their mobile devices ten hours a day, with men trailing slightly behind. In China, Internet addiction rehab centers are in great demand. In the ABCNews article "Chinese Teen Dies at Internet Addiction Rehab Camp," they note that China's National People's Congress believes that 10 percent of those under eighteen have an Internet addiction.

What gives when you give more to these activities? First, your sleep is deprived. We are trading our limited sleep time to respond to one more e-mail, watch one more cat video, or finish that Snapchat conversation. If that was not enough, study after study has shown that the blue glow these devices give off reduces our melatonin right before bed, which makes it harder to fall asleep as well as to enter our much-needed REM dream mode.

When you take your time investment inventory, mentioned at the beginning of this chapter, you will most likely find you are spending a great deal of time on unproductive and/or unfulfilling activities. As they say with any addiction, awareness and acceptance that you have a problem is the first step. No worries, you are in a big boat with many of us. There are many things you can do without having to enroll in an Internet addiction clinic.

First, realize that you may never be able to go cold turkey on all the activities that suck up your time, nor do you necessarily want to. However, you can take steps to mitigate their impact on your personal life, and often your work life. I like to borrow the eco slogan "reduce, reuse, recycle" and apply it to this process.

Reduce. List all the unproductive activities on which you waste your time; then, pick one, just one, that you can give up for one week. If that is too hard, give it up for one day. A good way to do this if you are a multi-device holder is to let the least essential mobile device battery die out and then put that device in a drawer. Extend your activity hiatus from one day to one week to one month. After one month, you will find it is much easier to leave it altogether. At the same time, make a pledge that you will not take on another unproductive activity or mobile device unless you drop one.

Until you reduce, you need to schedule time on the calendar that you will spend on these activities. Yes, mark your calendar to watch TV. This action will mentally bring these activities from your unconscious to your conscious mind. Over time, you will naturally reduce the time you spend on them. For those activities that rely on your friends or colleagues, such as texting, you need to tell them your schedule. Send a simple message that says, "I will respond to texts between 4 and 4:30 p.m. If you need me to respond sooner, please call me."

Reuse. Sometimes we can leverage (or reuse in a more valuable way) our unproductive activities to help us accomplish those goals we constantly have on our resolution list. As an addict of video games, I found that hours could pass before I even raised my head from the computer or iPad in front of me, yet I strained to spend just thirty minutes on the elliptical. So what did I do?

I propped an iPad up on the elliptical, turned on my game, and started exercising. I would wonder why I was soaking wet in such a short time, then realize I had been going for the past fifty-three minutes, nonstop. Many friends of mine have done this with TV. They binge-watch *Game of Thrones* while on the treadmill. There is a reason so many gyms have TVs attached to their aerobic equipment. You can also reuse your addictions as rewards. You get fifteen minutes more on Facebook if you cut the lawn or clean the bathroom, or, better yet, spend thirty minutes conversing undistracted with a loved one. What time waster can you reuse to make yourself more productive or increase your fulfillment?

Recycle. When it comes to Internet communication, there are literally thousands of ways for you to send the same message. Many people are posting the same vacation selfie to a multitude of social sites, such as Facebook, Instagram, Snapchat, Google+, Twitter, and so on. When it comes to recycling, look for programs that will put all your social media in one place. An aggregator I like to use is Hootsuite. There are many out there, and this was just the first one I fell upon. One message with the same pic can be posted to all your social media forums. Recycle the same message, photo, or text across all of these media.

Car tires are routinely recycled into some amazing things, from playground mats to safety cones to septic system liners. If you look at the list of popular time wasters I discussed above, you will find that many of them concern technology devices. Be creative in the ways you recycle these devices to better your life. Old, large TVs have been recycled as aquariums, while flat-screen TVs are used to display priceless paintings or messages. A friend of mine has her TV randomly display messages such as "Have you hugged your child today?" or "Name one thing you are grateful for right at this moment," or "Stop, just stop and breathe." I have recycled my old iPhone for use as a radio that plays background music while I write. It acts as my early warning signal to anyone walking by that I am busy writing.

Time addictions typically sneak up on you, often masquerading as time savers, ways to connect to people, or relaxing downtime. Let's be perfectly clear on the downtime part: any neurologist will tell you that your brain needs some downtime to refresh, but that does not come when you are mentally connected to an electronic device. So that hour you spent watching reruns of *Happy Days* while shopping on Amazon is just tricking you into thinking you are relaxing. Even exercise apps have a way of adding to your neural overload.

My Jawbone fitness tracker was a well-intended gadget because it raised my awareness of how much movement I was doing. It seemed like a good idea to put on the idle alert, so the wristband would let me know when I had been idle for more than thirty minutes. It also had a sleep tracker, which allowed me to view my sleep patterns. Oh, you can also put in your other exercise, to get a better idea of your entire fitness routine.

The tracker would congratulate me on my progress and then push me to do more. I was checking it when I woke up to view my sleep and then after a workout to log in the exercise. I would wonder how many steps I took for my morning walk. When I forgot to put my Jawbone on in the morning, I would literally shake it back and forth until the device logged my steps, even though I knew I had taken them. With all of the info and add-ons, it became a bit of an addiction for me. I also had to charge it every week. I decided to track the amount of time I was spending with this gizmo that was supposed to add value to my life. I thought it was taking me only a few minutes a week, while in reality I was spending thirty to forty minutes each week just looking at and inputting the data. It now sits in my desk drawer as an example of how something that appeared to be a minimal investment of time crept up on me, taking away two hours of my life every month.

Minding Now

I wondered what I could have done with those two hours per month I spent on the Jawbone, and also what I was interrupting in order to view the data. *Minding now* is all about realizing we have precious little time at home. By taking an inventory of your time, you will quickly understand the things that are taking you away from now. One question I like to ask myself is, "What is the most important thing you could be doing right now that would...?" Fill in the dots with your unique priority, such as "help me connect with my spouse" or "add value to my life" or "make me a healthier and happier person."

Multitasking has become prevalent in our busy lives. Studies and common sense tell you that you can do a task better when you give it your total focus than when you are doing it in conjunction with many other things. When was the last time you went to an orchestra and saw the cellist watching TV while performing? Or a pro basketball player texting while on the court? Yes, these are absurd examples, but they do get the point across. We perform best when we are focused, not multitasking. This approach extends to building, maintaining, or growing our relationships. A five-minute conversation without any interruptions and given full attention from both people will be far better than a thirty-minute conversation while one or both people are multitasking.

My favorite conversation time (as well as the shortest) of the day with my spouse is our morning dog walk together. There are no device interruptions and we can fully focus on our discussion. It helps to be in the countryside, where cell coverage is spotty at best. Our dog fully adheres to minding now. She is in the moment with a smell trail or seeking an opportune moment to chase a squirrel. An easy mnemonic is the word NOW:

- **No distractions.** Keep everything turned off, muted, and out of arm's reach.
- **Own it.** This is your time, so make sure, whether you are engaging with someone else or doing something by yourself, that you tell those around you that you want uninterrupted time.
- **Watch for results.** When you are fully present with a loved one, is your relationship better? Do you feel better? When you are truly present, is the time spent more memorable? Does it have a lasting impact on you?

Does all the time you spend have to be focused? The quick answer is no. Go ahead and watch some TV while you text selfies. However, be mindful of the time you spend in multitask mode and specifically set aside times when you are in the now. Also, be aware of the special moments you want to be fully there, such as a child's recital or the conversation at dinnertime. You cannot always control what others are doing, but you can influence them when you are fully present and minding now. Your limited time in life goes far quicker than you realize.

Whether you are managing priorities, mitigating addictions, or minding now, fully expect that you will not be perfect. You will slip and fall; we all do. Those who are successful at achieving and retaining a healthy balance in their personal lives have a plan to get back up if they fall. For some this is easier than it is for others. As I have spoken about throughout the chapters, work–life balance falls differently on us as individuals with different group memberships: whether you are a parent or non-parent, man or woman, young or old, you will have a unique perspective on work–life balance. In the next chapter I will speak to how a person's specific group membership can create challenges for maintaining work–life balance.

Discussion Points

- If you were to ask your loved one the three things he or she believes distracts you from being present, what would they be?
- How could you minimize these distractions?
- What value would you receive by minimizing these distractions?

Takeaways

- ✓ We can be addicted to activities that provide little or no value.
- ✓ To avoid losing the present, you should find ways to mind NOW.
- ✓ Prioritize those activities that provide you the most benefit and support your personal purpose.
- ✓ Go environmental with your time: reduce, reuse, and recycle.

Chapter 6

Inclusive Aspects of Work–Life Balance

If it is a people challenge, then inclusion should be part of the solution.

M y professional interest in the subject of diversity and inclusion is reflected in our decades of work helping companies create inclusive environments. I believe diversity and inclusion—D&I—provide an important lens for understanding work–life balance. I have seen how inattention to work–life balance has created a barrier to achieving diversity and inclusion goals. For leaders, I know this is a pressing issue as you attempt to create market differentiation and expand into new markets. I have devoted this chapter to inclusion and how work–life balance can either foster or challenge an inclusion initiative.

How does a diversity and inclusion initiative benefit from a focus on work–life balance? To the extent that a D&I initiative is about understanding the best ways to engage an increasingly diverse workforce, work–life balance is critical. Work–life balance needs will vary across diverse groups. When I joined corporate America, employee benefits programs were undergoing an overhaul. The concept of flex, or cafeteria, benefits was being embraced by more and more employers. These new benefits plans allowed employees to choose their benefits, customizing them to their personal needs, at least to some extent.

Flex plans represented perhaps the first widespread work–life balance program. It was an important step, in that the typical benefits policies up to that point reflected some very traditional assumptions: that employees were part of a nuclear family in which the parents were married, with a husband employed in the workplace and a wife working at home and raising children. The workforce, as noted in the Bureau of Labor's 1985 report *Workforce 2000*, was about to undergo a rapid demographic change, with more women entering the workforce, as well as more immigrants, more employees with nontraditional families, and more people with diverse spiritual practices. Generational diversity was also increasing, and fully four generational cohorts have been active in the workplace since the year 2000. It was becoming clear then, as it is so very clear now, that employers that are more able to respond to the needs of increasingly diverse workers will have an advantage. The more competitive the search for talent, the more important this advantage has become. Thus, work–life balance initiatives can be a source of competitive advantage in an increasingly diverse employment marketplace.

Dimensions that Make a Difference

For a while, balancing time between work and personal life was looked at as primarily a gender issue. The rationale was something like this: "Women are becoming more career oriented, there are more of them in the workplace, and they have a lot of challenges in balancing the needs of family. Thus, we need to help them better balance work and personal life." The framing of work–life balance as primarily a gender issue misses a number of important inclusion opportunities. Work–life balance is indeed an inclusion issue, but it encompasses many groups besides women.

So far, I have talked about balancing personal and work life as an issue for every individual and every company. I believe this is true. It matters not which group identities you hold; finding balance will enhance your engagement, productivity, satisfaction, and life. When I am looking at this issue through the lens of diversity and inclusion, though, a big opportunity emerges. Our ability to achieve optimal results is often related to our most important group identities.

I remember the cover of a magazine, perhaps *Life* or *Time*, in about 1990, emblazoned with the headline "The 25-Year-Olds"— the article talked about a critical generational shift related to workplace values. These twenty-five-year-olds were generation X, the generation that followed the baby boomers. The article discussed the very different values and attitudes the gen Xers held about their relationship with work and the workplace. They had more boundaries between work life and personal time, and they weren't as willing to work the endless hours that their boomer colleagues did. They were even a bit cynical, given the broken bargain they saw between their parents and their parents' employers, a bargain that implied lifelong employment in return for loyalty and good work. That bargain fell apart in the era of deregulation, competition, and emerging globalization in the 1980s. We see the results of this generation's perspective in today's parental leave policies, which give more room for fathers to participate in raising children.

Generational difference continues to be an important shaper

of workplace policies. Millennials continue what their gen X colleagues (and parents) started, by blurring the lines between work time and personal time. Millennials are known for multi-tasking, which sometimes means that work and personal time are not separate but rather one in the same. A study by Ernst & Young noted in the *Harvard Business Review* article "How Gen Y and Boomers Will Reshape Your Agenda," found that there is a quite a gap in the experiences and attitudes of baby boomers, who often hold senior leadership position, and millennials.

Recent research by Virtuali's *Develop the Next Gen* study shows that 28 percent of millennials fear taking leadership roles due to a deterioration in their work–life balance needs. Organizations that have a better understanding of the needs and perspectives of millennials, and offer them the room to manage their lives in the way they see fit, will have a huge advantage at a time when most large companies are competing even harder for talent and needing to get more from that talent in an increasingly competitive marketplace.

Millennials are just one of the groups that benefits when a diversity and inclusion lens is applied to programs designed to achieve a systemic culture of healthy work–life balance. There are a number of other groups that will also benefit, and thus these employees will be easier to recruit, more engaged, and more productive. These groups today include, but are not limited to:

- Gender
- Generation
- Religious minorities
- People living with disabilities
- Caregivers

This list includes many of the traditional "outsider" or "minority" groups that have not been fully utilized in many large companies. The challenges outsider groups face go beyond work–life balance, but do include this complex issue. Thus, the opportunity exists for companies to increase inclusion and engagement by constructing a balanced culture. It is not surprising that organizations are focusing on the needs of "outsider" groups. The very definition of "outsiderness" reflects a dynamic in which the needs and perspectives of certain groups are assumed, not understood, not valued, and/or not considered.

Core Diversity and Inclusion Dynamics

To understand the intersection of inclusiveness and work–life balance, and their interaction with "outsiderness," you need to understand and control for the two most fundamental diversity and inclusion dynamics: unconscious bias and insider–outsider dynamics. These are detailed in a book I coauthored , *The Inclusion Dividend*, but I will provide a short overview here. Inclusive leadership is about managing these dynamics by (1) controlling for unconscious bias and (2) minimizing the impact of insider–outsider dynamics.

Unconscious bias is essentially about how the brain works. Our brains categorize information, store it in our unconscious, and then tap into it to make decisions. According to Nobel Prize winner Daniel Kahneman, the vast majority of the decisions we make are influenced by our acquired assumptions without us being particularly aware that these assumptions have impacted our decision. For example, your daily commute home involves dozens of little decisions that you are largely unaware of, because you have made those decisions so many times that they don't require conscious thought. It is these decisions that are most likely to reflect unconscious bias, as some of the data stored in our unconscious brains contains stereotypes and assumptions that are inaccurate and biased. These assumptions and stereotypes affect the way individuals view and treat groups of people. These dynamics have to be controlled and minimized by the organization if a balance initiative is to resonate with an increasingly diverse workforce.

In some ways, the view of work–life balance as a gender issue reflects our unconscious (or sometimes conscious) biases, as we associate women with the responsibilities of primary caregiver at home for either children or adults. This bias plays out in the way managers conduct interviews with women, dole out project assignments, and consider career advancement opportunities.

In an attempt to create a more inclusive talent acquisition process for one of our clients, one of the managers volunteered to have his interviews recorded and audited. Interviewees were told the interview was recorded for educational purposes and had a chance to decline the recording; none of them did. While auditing interviews for a financial position, I noticed that this well-intentioned manager, who only wanted the best employee, would change his conversation depending upon the gender of the interviewee. When he interviewed women, he brought up the subject of flextime and work–life balance several times and highlighted it throughout the interview. When he interviewed men, the matter was seldom discussed. Even when one male candidate asked about the work–life balance culture, the manager gave a short reply and changed the subject. When I approached the manager about this change in talk, he did not believe he emphasized such issues more with one gender or the other... until he listened to the recording of the interviews, and his mouth fell open. Upon reflection, he just assumed work–life balance was a top issue for women but not for men. The company's candidate survey data, however, showed that career advancement was the priority for women, and work–life balance was often in the top two for men.

The association of a particular challenge with just one group of people also reflects insider–outsider dynamics. Insider–outsider dynamics both create and result from the different experiences and power of various groups within a national, societal, and even global context. Handedness gives us a good metaphor. Ask a group of left-handed people what it means to be left-handed, and they will likely provide a long list of the ways they have had to adapt to a right-handed world, naming everything from sports equipment, to school desks, to handwriting. Ask right-handed people what it means to be right-handed and you will get blank stares. They are the insiders, the group with more power, and thus the group that doesn't need to see its "groupness." Lefties are the outsiders, the group that needs to understand its groupness in order to fit in and be successful. While outsiders are aware of the difference, and are aware of the power difference between their group and the insider group, insiders don't see groups and don't see an issue; they just see individuals who happen to be either left- or right-handed.

The linking of work–life balance in the workplace with women reflects insider–outsider dynamics in that the insider group (men) prefers to see gender issues as being about women and their struggles to manage a complicated life and its demands; they tend to underplay or not see the role that men play in benefiting from biases that make it more difficult for women to succeed in the workplace. To achieve full awareness across this particular gender dynamic would require men having to see themselves as a group that benefits from bias, something that most insider groups find difficult. Insider–outsider dynamics have a strong influence over the work–life balance policies that are developed, as the insider group's assumptions and needs usually drive policy, just as right-handers' do.

So, how does understanding these core dynamics allow us to leverage the opportunity presented by addressing work–life balance? Quite simply, the better we understand the experiences of outsider groups, the better we can address their unique work-place challenges. In order to do this, we have to overcome the insider–outsider dynamics, which tend to reflect tradition and the perspective of the insider group, as well as unconscious (or conscious) bias, which creates limiting or inaccurate assumptions. A fully implemented inclusive initiative geared to reducing these negative dynamics of difference will have to address work–life balance as a challenge that requires a solution that benefits every group. Understanding the dynamics of inclusion will allow us to challenge and break through assumptions and better address these challenges and opportunities.

Gender

As I said earlier, my interest in work–life balance came from our firm's decades of helping companies leverage their diversity by creating a more inclusive workplace. We noticed a pattern. If you start a conversation about gender in the workplace, the conversation will quickly turn to balancing personal and professional life, work and home, having and raising children. Work–life balance has been viewed as inherently a gender issue. Better said, it was often viewed as the most prevalent gender issue, and a convenient off-ramp that avoided a more difficult conversation about gender. This off-ramp circumvented the core of the gender challenge, which is about the inclusion and engagement of women that result from a reduction of unconscious (or conscious) bias in day-to-day behaviors and the bias embedded in the systemic policies, procedures, and norms.

Let's be clear, work–life balance is an issue for women, but it's not the only issue and it's not the most important issue. It is also an issue for men, but again, it's not the only issue and it's not the most important issue. When women feel free to candidly answer questions about why they leave companies, they often cite other challenges, such as the culture of the organization, as the main reason for their departure. Work–life balance is rarely at the top of the list.

Work–life balance is on the list of priorities, however. Our ability to address the intersection of gender and healthy work–life balance will increase the inclusion and engagement of women. Again, this issue must not be seen as a panacea for sexism but instead as one way to improve women's experience in the workplace. So how can organizations use work–life balance policies to increase the engagement of both men and women? With the proper engagement that reflects options, assumptions, and positioning, an organization can craft a more inclusive solution.

Options

It is far too easy to see one solution as one size fits all, especially if you are gearing that solution solely toward one group of people. For example, as mentioned in an earlier chapter, wheelchair ramps were initially designed specifically for those in wheelchairs. And they were very helpful in increasing access for those in wheelchairs. However, the ramps became a benefit to everyone from the person wheeling a stroller to the UPS driver with a dolly to the person who had hurt himself temporarily. For the most part, people just refer to them as ramps now instead of the oft-stated wheelchair ramp.

Technology, work-space, and vacation policies that promote a healthier work–life balance should be geared to an inclusive audience and provide options. For example, a parental leave policy can be geared to allow for caregivers who have new children (either by birth or adoption) as well as those who take on the care of their parents. In our changing times, family life policies that provide options require a greater outreach to both genders.

Assumptions

Two-way communication between the employee and the organization is critical. Work–life balance policies can be used to communicate a broader array of options to women and parents in general. Although women are physically bearing children, more and more men are becoming primary caretakers. If a company is committed to full engagement of its employees, it needs to view the work of having and raising children as a normal event, and support it with practices and policies.

Focus on the big picture, which is a talent development landscape that goes further than the year that it takes many parents to adjust to the significant changes that having children brings. The operating assumption should be that caring for a family member is a normal part of an employee's career (men and women), not an off-ramp that reduces career opportunities. All employees should be evaluated based on their entire work experience, and their career trajectory should reflect this perspective.

Positioning

The family-related challenges that caregivers face are often seen as women's challenges. Position work–life balance as benefiting men and women. This takes the negative (from a career perspective) spotlight off women, and has the potential to increase the engagement of men. Many men are also balancing family needs and aren't supported in even articulating their struggles and needs from this perspective. In fact, Ernst & Young's *Global Generations Research* found that 80 percent of millennials are in relationships in which both partners work, and balancing the personal side of their lives is a big concern. By contrast, only 47 percent of baby boomers are in dual-income relationships. Because boomers tend to hold the corporate power positions, this disparity creates a gap in experience and knowledge that is reflected in policy and practice, and maintained by insider–outsider dynamics.

By failing to approach childbearing and child-rearing in a positive and inclusive manner, organizations create a self-fulfilling prophecy whereby women who don't really want to slow or end their careers do so anyhow because they don't feel supported by the organization. When these women leave they often report that they want to spend more time with their children, although the research points to other reasons for their departure. This reinforces the stereotype and feeds the self-fulfilling prophecy. It is essential to take thoughtful action connected to a long-term strategy to manage talent.

We can address gender much more clearly and directly in an inclusive organization. The better we understand the challenges that women face and the role men play in those challenges, the more effective we can be in creating work–life balance strategies that support women in advancing in their careers in ways commensurate with their abilities.

Generations

The three, and sometimes four, generations currently in the workplace have very different views about how to balance work and personal life. Generally, older generations drew stricter lines between work and personal life. Research in the *Managing the Multigenerational Workforce* study from CompTIA, an IT trade association, found that generation X made work–life balance a legitimate pursuit and millennials continued that trend. This same study showed that millennials use their devices to blur the lines between work and personal life, as a part of their multitasking culture. In the eyes of older generations, the desire of millennials to multitask and blur the lines between work and personal life is evidence of a lower work ethic and a lack of focus and commitment. For millennials, these behaviors reflect their commitment to their work and their desire to work efficiently. In order to use work–life balance to create better engagement of diverse generational cohorts, organizations should focus on the following definition and support.

Definition

As a leader, do not define work–life balance from the perspective of the older generation, which sees the issue as a matter of setting traditional boundaries. Because generation X and, to some extent, late baby boomers are in the "insider" group when it comes to age, their view of work styles will hold sway. They tend to view millennials as less committed and unwilling to work hard, and this becomes a conscious and sometimes unconscious bias. This is ironic because millennials are hardworking and very practical. Using the boomer and gen X paradigm results in millennials feeling pressed to adjust to these traditional norms to avoid being seen in a negative light. This decreases engagement and productivity, and can increase turnover.

Support

A client of mine, during the dot-com boom, needed to employ a lot of programmers and tech specialists in order to take advantage of a big market opportunity. The corporate culture was so traditional and conservative that the company had to create a different set of policies and practices for its new employees, and it even put this new department in a separate building. These employees, many of them early millennials, wanted a more flexible schedule. Hard work was not an issue, but they wouldn't work well if they were given a traditional schedule. Sometimes they wanted to come in at 10 a.m. and sometimes they wanted to leave at 1 a.m. They needed more flexible access to technology. They needed to be allowed to use their expertise in a way that maximized their contribution to the business.

The company's business needs forced it to figure out a way to meet these new employees' demands. Perhaps it was the best strategy at that time. However, most organizations are now at a place where more flexible policies and practices can be extended to the whole organization, wherever practical. Lack of flexibility is one reason many millennials quit their jobs. A November 6, 2015, *Wall Street Journal* article, "Goldman Sachs Sweetens Deal for Young Bankers," speaks to the way Goldman had to radically rethink its working policies for millennial recruits. The challenge was not securing smart, engaged employees, it was retaining them. Goldman is not alone. The banking industry is struggling to redefine its traditional late hours and weekend work culture for junior associates. Other industries, including the Silicon Valley technology sector, are luring the younger generation with their nontraditional cultures, which better reflect millennials' lifestyle needs.

Sometimes the path to the solution involves questioning "traditions," which often reflect embedded biases. Does all work need to be accomplished between nine in the morning and five in the evening? Can work be project based instead of time based? Is the current corporate structure, with its ever-increasing hierarchy, best for today's workforce? Some companies, such as Zappos and Amazon, are addressing these questions and others. They are not only disrupting the traditional approach, which favored one particular group, but are becoming widely successful in doing so. As of this writing, Amazon has surpassed Walmart, with its very traditional corporate structure, as the largest retailer. Zappos is experimenting with eliminating its entire management structure in favor of a more hive-oriented culture. Both companies need to focus more on work–life balance culture, but at least they have taken an approach that allows them to prevent tradition from reaching their goals: engaging their ever-changing workforce. Neither Amazon or Zappos will tell you it is easy. In fact, it has caused a lot of controversy in and out of their companies. However, they will both most likely tell you it is a journey they needed to embark on to be a future market leader.

Living with Disabilities

At a societal level, there is both unemployment and underemployment of people living with disabilities. Some of this is structural and some is attitudinal. Work–life balance policies can indirectly impact the attitudinal challenges that people living with disabilities face. These attitudinal challenges reflect the still strong stereotypes that people living with disabilities are less intelligent and less capable. This is a lost opportunity that can be at least partially addressed through balance strategies. There are two core issues to consider from a practical perspective. One is ensuring that there is enough flexibility and support for employees to manage the physical challenges related to their disabilities. The other is providing enough flexibility in ways of working to maximize the participation of individuals living with mental challenges that are reflected in different learning needs.

The ADA (Americans with Disabilities Act) is comprehensive in its directives to create reasonable accommodation: it demands strong, compliance-based change, and is absolutely necessary to ensure equitable treatment of people living with disabilities. However, who is interested in just being "accommodated"? The sense is similar to that of diversity policies and programs that speak to "tolerance." Who wants to be "tolerated"? Most of us want to be included. Full engagement of people with disabilities requires a more proactive approach. The full suite of flexibility options has the potential to be beneficial to people living with disabilities.

The U.S. Department of Labor suggests that work–life balance strategies for people living with disabilities should focus on three areas: time, or work schedule; place, or where the work gets done; and task, or the type of work.

One company that has made serious advancements in this area is Target. While shopping there recently I asked an associate where something was located. I hailed the first person in a red shirt I found. The gentleman I asked was deaf. He had a prerecorded message on the iPhone he carried that said he was deaf but would like to help me. I just had to ask my question into his phone and it automatically converted my speech into text. He was then able to take me quickly to the right location. It dawned on me later that I have never encountered a deaf person working on the floor in a retail environment. Target did not allow hearing impairment to be a barrier in the workplace. With minimal device support this employee was able to perform the same tasks as anyone else. Applying this idea to the work–life balance strategy, a company could consider a flextime initiative for those who require special transportation or regular medical visits.

Spiritual Diversity

The insider–outsider dynamic at play around spiritual practice means that most Western-based organizations' policies assume one spiritual practice—usually Christianity. For those who are not Christian, there may be constant adjustments made by the employee. A policy based only on a dominant group is often seen as giving a special advantage to that religious group.

As corporations become more global, their customers and employees become more diverse. Many religions require the observance of holidays, meal restrictions, and daily rituals. A company's approach to time off for holidays can be a challenge to those who are not part of the religious majority. A number of companies are adopting a more flexible option that provides an allotment of personal days that employees can use for their holiday observances instead of being given holidays based on Christian observances such as Christmas and Easter. These forced holidays require employees who observe different holidays to use their vacation leave.

Even the traditional workweek is based upon observance of holy days, such as Sunday for Christians. For Muslims, the holy day is Friday and for Jews it is Saturday. Some companies cannot change their workweek due to industry-wide schedules, such as the opening of markets or local work laws that may require businesses to remain closed on certain days. As a leader, keeping an open mind and providing options when possible will go a long way toward ensuring greater work–life balance for a diverse religious workforce.

As I mentioned earlier, policies geared toward increasing work–life balance for one group may extend to serve multiple groups in sometimes unpredictable ways. For example, in chapter 4 I suggested designating a quiet room that could serve as a place for employees to take a "mindful minute" or have a clean, private place to attend to medical needs. This room can also serve as a quiet place for those whose religions require daily prayers. It is a great example of how one work–life balance solution can have an inclusive impact on a diverse group of employees.

Inclusive Outcome

The benefits of an inclusive approach to work–life balance are many, both at the individual and organizational levels. What was initially viewed as a zero-sum game—meaning, the more I give to one group, the more I have to take from other groups—is now being seen as an approach that benefits all groups, and thus the organization. Think of the saying, "A rising tide lifts all boats."

Consider the policies and practices that evolved as the result of efforts over the last twenty-five years to increase the inclusion of people living with physical disabilities. Following the passage of the Americans with Disabilities Act of 1991 there were many changes: accessible entrances, cut curbs on sidewalks, ramps, and larger bathroom stalls among them. Who benefits from these changes? Many of us benefit from them all the time. I am constantly rolling my suitcase around cities, in and out of parking lots, and am on the constant lookout for the cut curbs. I often want to change my clothes quickly at an airport and I benefit from the larger stall. I suspect most of us benefit from these changes every day, whether or not we are living with a disability.

It is important for all of us to realize that everyone benefits from inclusiveness. Men benefit from the increased inclusion of women, which has created more flexible policies. Heterosexuals have benefited from domestic-partner benefits policies. Cross-cultural fluency has helped many of us in the U.S. be more successful selling our services. People of all spiritual practices benefit from increased flexibility for religious practice in the workplace.

Work–life balance is an inclusion issue in that it does affect every identity group and perhaps every individual in every workplace. One challenge of diversity and inclusion proponents over the last couple of decades has been to educate people about how D&I efforts make life better for everyone, not just specific groups. The question "What is in it for me?" has been answered by outsider groups, but not so much by insider groups. However, D&I initiatives that are seemingly geared toward creating a better work environment for particular groups actually benefit all employees.

The challenges of work–life balance are somewhat different in terms of impact and action for workplaces characterized by an increasingly diverse group of people, people who are diverse in many ways and represent a large number of important affinity and identity groups. The best solution relates to what we actually see and understand about diverse groups present in the organization.

Kenji Yoshino, in his book *Covering: The Hidden Assault on Our Civil Rights,* speaks to the price paid when employees are unable to be themselves at work, when they cover up important aspects of who they are. This dynamic can affect engagement, retention, productivity, and innovation. Yoshino also speaks to the opportunities that emerge when employees have room to be who they are. A proper focus on work–life balance makes a strong contribution to creating the kind of flexibility and inclusion that are becoming ever more critical to large corporations. If an organization faces a people challenge, inclusion should be part of the solution.

Discussion Points

- Where have you noted work–life balance being viewed as a challenge for just one particular group?
- What happens when work–life balance solutions are geared just for that group?
- How could these solutions be geared to support a diversity and inclusion initiative?

Takeaways

✓ Work–life balance is a challenge for everyone.
✓ Solutions can provide value to an inclusive workforce.

✓ Sometimes work–life balance can come down to options. Provide them.

✓ Remove tradition as a barrier to creating a healthier work–life culture.

✓ Question your assumptions about particular groups and solutions crafted for those groups.

Conclusion

One apple grows from two different trees.

Most people do not know that an apple, golden or otherwise, is typically grown from technically two different trees. In order to ensure a healthy apple tree that propagates the exact apple you are seeking, a branch of the selected apple tree is grafted onto the root stock of a different apple tree. The root stock determines the height of the tree as well as the soil in which it will grow best, while the branch graft is focused on the fruit.

Why is this idea important in achieving a healthy work–life balance? Think of the root stock as the systemic foundation, or, in the business sense, the corporate structure, policies, and norms. Each branch can be seen as a business unit that splits off to departments and then to teams and finally to the individuals, the apples. You cannot grow a healthy crop of apples without giving attention to the entire tree, from the roots on up.

In order for the tree to weather storms, blights, and other external attacks, there needs to be a holistic sustainment strategy. The same can be said for sustaining a culture that promotes healthy work–life balance. In order for the corporation to thrive amid market fluctuations, competition, and employee burnout, there needs to be a sustainment strategy that goes beyond one-time development or simple policy change. Just as we look to the two different parts of the apple tree, we must look at the two major influences that impact balance: individual behavior and systemic influence. Focusing on one and not the other will bear short-term results at best.

So what is needed to sustain a healthy work–life culture that incorporates an inclusive solution for everyone? It can be summed up using APPLE as a mnemonic: align, presence, plan, live, and engage.

Align

At the start of this book I spoke directly to the way a misalignment of purpose, from the organizational down to the individual level, can create a barrier to finding workable solutions to work–life balance challenges. Establishing easy-to-understand and clear purposes for the organization, teams, and individuals will allow everyone to make the necessary tweaks to bring the entire culture into alignment.

When you take your car in for tire service, you cannot focus on aligning only three out of the four wheels; in time, that fourth poorly aligned wheel will pull every other wheel out of alignment. Even if your organizational and team purposes are in alignment (meaning they are symbiotic and each supports achievement of the other's goals), being unaware of your own purpose and/or your individual reports' purposes will cause a drag that will eventually drive the entire organization off the road to success.

Establish and communicate purpose at every level.

Presence

I struggled with the term *work–life balance,* as it has been over-used and thus often generalized to a point that creates mis-understanding. However, not using the term up front risks disconnecting this book from the audience I am trying to help. If I had my druthers, I would call the state I am trying to achieve *work–life presence.* So often, a healthy outlook is about being mentally and physically co-located. Research has shown this is becoming ever more pressing for our up-and-coming digital generations. It is far too easy to be physically in one place yet mentally somewhere else via our devices.

As I see the graduating masses ready to enter the work world, I am reminded of a June 1997 *Chicago Tribune* column by Mary Schmich, later adapted into a song, that said, "If I could offer you only one tip for the future, sunscreen would be it." I would change the line just a bit to say, "If I could offer you only one tip for the future, be present." Our lives, as much as our everyday commotion may try to hide it, are strikingly short. Our productive working piece of that life is even shorter. We do not have the luxury of directing our attention away from what is happening right in front of us with the promise that tomorrow will be different. Your direct reports respond better, are more engaged, and produce better results when you give them your full attention for the periods of time you are speaking or meet-ing with them. They will eventually mirror your behavior. Your relationships at home are richer and more fulfilling when you allocate times in which you will be fully present for your loved ones.

Practice presence. Be present.

Plan

It is all too easy to look at an employee engagement survey that shows there is an ever-growing concern over work–life balance, and to make one or two policy changes to fix it. History has shown these quick fixes bear dismal results in the long term, and can even worsen the situation. Leaders need to stop and create a plan that has a holistic short- and long-term strategy. They also need to be careful not to frame this issue as a women's or generational problem. As with any people strategy, the plan should have an inclusive approach that provides value to the full organization.

Any psychiatrist will tell you that a regimen that provides medication but no counseling will not offer a solution to regaining mental health. Policy and procedure changes without leadership development will not offer a solution to regaining a healthy work–life balance. The work–life balance plan needs to look at what can be changed at a systemic level but also at what will be needed in terms of individual behavior to effect the change the organization seeks. For example, a work-from-home policy that does not provide development to leaders on how to manage remote team members, as well as development to those working from home on how to create personal and work boundaries, will invariably lead to serious challenges.

Develop a holistic plan before making any changes.

Live

Sounds like an odd guide, eh? Well, there is a difference between being alive and living. Understand that work is a major part of your life. Find ways to make it work for you and your team. The term *work–life* sometimes makes it seem that they are two separate entities. You have a personal life and a work life. It is not uncommon for them to blend together in a healthy way. Many people find their spouses at work. Our colleagues can become lifelong friends, remaining in our lives even after we are no longer working under the same roof. If work is what you need to do to fulfill your personal purpose, then invest fully in it when you are there. Living your work life means you are present, fully connected, and understand the value it brings you as well as those around you. Living your personal life can be viewed in exactly the same manner. Do not let either one slip by without squeezing every drop of value out of it. It is not always a matter of how many hours we spend in one or the other, but how we spend that time when we are there.

Be respectful of your team's personal lives. If they are on vacation, do everything you can to build a wall around them so they can fully disconnect. Before you send an e-mail at 11 p.m., ask yourself if you would call at 11 p.m. for that same subject. If the answer is no, then hold off on the e-mail. Same goes for the weekends. If you allow your team to live their personal lives fully when they are out of the office, they are more likely to live their work lives fully when they are in the office.

Live your work life fully. Live your personal life fully.

Engage

Find ways for you and your team to connect with the three p's: *people, passion,* and *in person.* Okay, I cheated a bit on that last "p." Dunbar's law postulates that our cognitive limit for stable social relationships is around 150. Choose carefully. Do not fool yourself into thinking that the 300-plus "friends" you have on Facebook are actual friends. The same goes for work colleagues. Dunbar did not postulate that you have 150 relationships each in both work and personal life, but rather 150 in total. Some of us will be able to manage more, while for others the number will be less. If you fill your brain space and attention span viewing photos from someone you knew in first grade, but have never spoken to in person again and don't intend to speak to again, then you just lost one person you could create a real connection with. Protect your time and your team's time. Try to lasso committees, needless meetings, and extracurricular projects that do not bring value and end up being a time sink.

At work, the most important people to you as a manager should be your team, followed by your manager and peers. In your personal life, the most important people tend to be your family, friends, and neighbors, in that order. Make time to disconnect yourself from technology visits (liking, e-mailing, texting, etc.), so you can make in-person visits. The human brain starves for real-life stimulus where you can see, hear, touch, and even smell other people and pets. Studies have shown that simply petting a dog reduces your heart rate as well as the dog's.

That brings us to passion. Discover what your passion in life is. Is it art (painting, singing, acting, sculpting, drawing, music, etc.)? Maybe it is socially oriented, like sports, or more introverted, like gardening? What is the one thing you do that makes you lose track of time and feel fulfilled after you have completed it? Find it and make it an explicit part of your life. Discover how work helps you connect with this passion. As a leader, help your team discover how work supports their pursuit of their passion.

Engage with people in person.

Make the apple golden. Following the APPLE guidelines

above will help you, your team, and your family create a healthy work–life balance. It will not always be easy, nor will it be without slipups along the way. As a business owner, I have found myself stuck on one side of the work–life seesaw. My experience with the fitness tracker shows that life can fall out of balance slowly and despite the best of intentions. Sometimes it takes a trusted friend or colleague to alert you. Other times, something blindsides you on a sunny Thursday afternoon. In the midst of writing this book, I was diagnosed with skin cancer. Regardless of the type of cancer, the "c" word can freeze people in their tracks. Luckily for me, it is easily curable with surgery. Despite all my best intentions to write a book that would help people establish a better work–life balance, I was slowly but surely tipping my own balance more and more toward work to meet writing deadlines and client demands.

The diagnosis call from the doctor was followed by more than a mindful minute. It caused me to reassess goals and sometimes constructed emergencies. A call to my publisher got my publishing date moved from spring to fall. Taking an inventory of my time addictions allowed me to free up some mind space and time for a passion of mine, which is being outside. I scheduled hikes with my dog on the calendar. Writing is such a solitary task, I realized I was unnecessarily limiting my human contact, so I immediately reached out to friends and family to schedule dinners and weekend visits. I reassessed all my travel plans, and reduced my travel days by more than half. I declared a work travel sabbatical of sorts from June 1 to September 1. We scheduled a consultant retreat for all of our colleagues to spend time together and network in person. Saturdays were declared disconnected days, which meant no Internet, TV, or mobile phone use from sunup to sundown. This was difficult but incredibly freeing. It is amazing how much more time you have to engage your family, friends, and neighbors when you're not distracted by digital chatter.

It is troubling to see how willing we are, without noticing, to slip on the golden handcuffs. However, handcuffs, whether gold or iron, are simply restraints. They restrain us from being a great boss, engaged partner, and loving parent. Over time, they weigh on us mentally and physically, taking away from both work and personal life. The golden apple is a simple metaphor that shows we do not need to give up the benefits of our current situation, but we can choose to transform these handcuffs into something that brings value to our business, our team, and our family. Go ahead take a bite. It is delicious.

P.S. Reviews are helpful feedback not only for other readers, but also for the author. Please take the time to share what you think about this book by reviewing it online. Thanks!

Acknowledgments

The idea for the title, *The Golden Apple,* comes from my prior corporate sales experience, where the phrase "golden hand-cuffs" was used often. Many of us felt chained to our pay-checks. This book is rooted in my personal experience, but it is also greatly influenced by conversations and interactions with colleagues, clients, and friends. Many of the ideas have been fleshed out in the course of Dagoba Group's leadership devel-opment work to support a healthy work–life balance. Sincere thanks goes to Amber Mayes, who was instrumental in devel-oping the work–life balance leadership development as well as in providing helpful feedback on the initial iterations of this book. Mark Kaplan, who has been an amazing coauthor on both *The Inclusion Dividend* and *SET for Inclusion,* graciously lent his expertise in the inclusion chapter and offered editorial assis-tance. This book would not have come as far as it did without his continual support.

This is our third book with Bibliomotion for a specific rea-son. They are a fantastic publisher who provides a welcome partnership throughout the writing journey. It may seem ironic that writing a book on work–life balance would challenge the author's work–life balance. All books have deadlines, rewrites, and various process pressures. It was my friends and family who helped me live the life I was preaching. It is a balance, and we need a strong support network to keep it in check. Life is too short not to enjoy it, in and out of work. A round of gratitude to everyone who was part of this process.

Index